8167

D1208236

FOOTBALL
BASICS

FOOTBALL BASICS

Jim Stillwagon, Toronto Argonauts
Tom Stillwagon, Miami of Ohio
Jim Young, British Columbia Lions
Zenon Andrusyshyn, Toronto Argonauts

Methuen

Toronto   London   Sydney   Wellington

ISBN   0-458-91160-7 hc
       0-458-91150-X pb

Photos: John Nelson
Illustrations: Estfin Enterprises

Printed and bound in Canada
by The Alger Press

1 2 3 4 5   78 77 76 75 74

INTRODUCTION

George Gross, The Toronto Sun

A "how-to" book in the basics of Canadian football is a welcome addition to sports literature in North America. For the first time the coach, amateur and fan in Canada will have a ready guide to his game. It is a unique football book in that it explains the mechanics and finesse required in the three most important facets of the game today; line play, pass receiving and kicking. Whether you are a football novice or an avid Saturday afternoon armchair quarterback, the book will both enlighten you and give an added appreciation of the finer points of the game.

DEFENSIVE LINE PLAY

Jim Stillwagon, Toronto Argonauts

JIM STILLWAGON

Jim Stillwagon is a defensive tackle with the Toronto Argonauts in the Canadian Football League. He is a 1971 graduate of Ohio State University and received his Bachelor of Science degree in Public Recreation.

Some honors Stillwagon received while at Ohio State were: outstanding freshman lineman, co-captain of the 1970 team, most valuable player on the Ohio State football team his senior year, All Big Ten 1969, 1970, first recipient of the Vince Lombardi Block of Granite trophy as outstanding college lineman, Knute Rockne Trophy as best lineman in the United States, awarded the Outland Trophy as the outstanding interior lineman in university ranks. Stillwagon was consensus All-American for 2 years, 1969 and 1970. He was named to the 50-year All Rose Bowl team. Stillwagon was drafted by the Green Bay Packers in the fifth round.

WHAT IT TAKES TO BE A LINEMAN

The lineman is an individual who must want satisfaction out of personal accomplishment on the field. He will only be recognized through consistent effort. The lineman must constantly discipline and prepare himself in the off season to be physically and mentally ready for the season.

The football game of today has become so specialized that we forget the two fundamental routines that have been an essential part of the game from its inception—blocking and tackling. If the player can do these well, the game will be a little easier for him to excel in.

To me a football team is like a machine or a carpenter's tool box. Each part is vital to the accomplishment of the job; it just depends on which part of the machine or which tool you want to be. If you want to be a lineman you must have an instinct to achieve goals. The defensive lineman must enjoy breaking double-team blocks, whipping the man over him, beating the crack-down blocks, standing up and defeating the iso back, tying up line play and preventing a run, defeating the pulling guards and tackles so the runner has no interference in front of him, and harassing the quarterback so his timing is off, making him pull down and scramble so the defense can sack him. These are the goals a defensive lineman must achieve to make the game worthwhile.

The offensive lineman must take pride in himself and keep in mind what is necessary in accomplishing team goals. He must want to have a high percentage of blocking efficiency, dominate the defensive player in the offensive running and passing game, never miss an assignment, and make key blocks to spring the ball carrier for long gains. These are the goals an offensive lineman must set for himself.

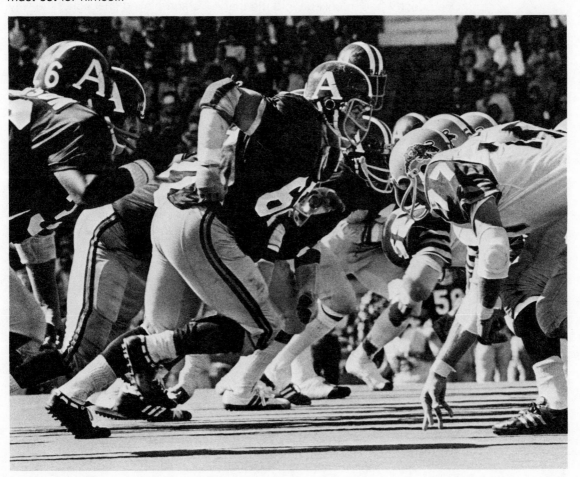

When I was young I remember being told to do everything above average. There are a lot of average people in the world, but not many above average. I have tried to follow that advice in everything I do. The first thing to do is to find out what the average is, then push yourself beyond that point. This will give you the discipline required to be a football player and the little extra effort when you need it. You gain more confidence knowing that you can go longer and harder than the opposition. This is the winning edge in football that will make you successful.

It is a myth to think that the lineman doesn't have to think and make fast decisions. The quarterback or backs have a few seconds to diagnose the defense and make up their minds on their individual patterns. The lineman, however, must react on the snap of the ball, make his block, determine which blocking technique is being used on him, find the flow of the play and carry out his responsibility. You cannot sit on the line and do nothing offensively or defensively unless you want to be manhandled.

BASICS OF DEFENSIVE PLAY

The best defense is to always be on the offense. The defense should force the offense out of what they can do best (their game plan) and put them into a position foreign to their style of play. *Surprise* is one of the keys to victory, and the defense can use this to their advantage by stunting, over-shifting, and camouflaging their coverage. But before they can do this, each defensive man must practice and be able to carry out basic fundamentals. Each man must know his position and responsibilities, be able to tackle, communicate with his teammates, and have the desire to win.

One coach I had in college told me that if his son played linebacker the way he told him to, he'd become a great linebacker. I believe that players must have the ability to perform in their position, but they must also be able to fit into the right type of defense player and work with the coaching staff. Only in this way will the cohesive team necessary to win the games be put together.

Defensive line play is brutal on you. First, you must ward off the offensive blocks and pursue the ball carrier through the traffic of both teams. Then you must stop.the momentum of the player carrying the ball at his running speed. During the game and the football season this becomes a demanding sequence.

But you must always stay with basics. Always key on the man directly over you or in your area. Defensive players get into trouble when they start watching the backfield motion. The purpose of backfield motion is to mislead you. The offensive player over you will give you a key to the type of play being run and where it is going, because like your offensive team, the defensive player will follow specific blocking procedure. If, for instance, the offensive man tries to cut you off to the inside you can be pretty sure that the play will be going inside, and vice versa. Also, it is easy to detect a pass play by the type of blocking.

Defensive Blocking

There are many types of blocking combinations that a defensive lineman can face. The offense has many weapons that it can throw at you. They have the advantage against the defense because they know where the play is going, what the snap count is going to be, and they usually only have to make contact on one individual. The defense can anticipate the play from the offensive formation, field position, down, and distance, and attempt to beat the offensive lineman off on the snap count. Half the battle is won if you can do this, and it is only by exploding off the ball and looking for individual keys from offensive personnel that you can accomplish it. Some keys include:

1. Change of weight from the feet to the hands indicates that a man is going to pull or that a passing play is coming.

2. An indication of nervous tension in the arms and a change of weight from the feet to the hands indicates that a straight-ahead block is coming.

3. The position of the offensive man's head may sometimes indicate whether a pass or run play is in the offing.

4. Alignment of the offensive line offers keys. If they line up wide apart, it could be that they are trying to get a little more room for a running play inside. When they line up close together, a pass or outside run could be coming.

5. The movement of the quarterback's hands and feet can give away the snap count, if you are in a position to see them.

6. The alignment of the backs can also give the play away. If the backs are cheated up to get into a good blocking position, you can expect a run. They usually spread apart to release out for a pass.

There are many individual keys you can pick up on your own that will give the snap count or play away. You just have to experience them yourself. Once you can master this, you can save yourself a lot of generated energy that can be used for another cause in the game.

Defeating Offensive Blocking

Defensive Weapons

1. hands

2. forearms

3. shoulders

4. head

In the offensive section of this book the offensive blocks have been diagrammed, and you are aware of the offender's assignment on each blocking situation. You have defensive weapons you can use to overcome these blocks—the hands, forearms, shoulders, and head. Following are ways in which to overcome the offender in specific blocking situations.

One-on-One Block

This is sometimes called the cut-off block. Territorial responsibility is very important in this situation—take care of your own area first. Use your physical strength and defensive weapons to neutralize and defeat the offensive man.

Two-on-One Block

Usually the inside blocker is the post man and the outside blocker is the driver. Defeat and neutralize the first man who blocks on you. Then split the gap between the blockers. If you get caught too high and out of leverage position, spin out with a seat roll, gather your feet under yourself, and find the ball. Never get driven back off the line of scrimmage. When this happens you get in your linebacker's way and create running room for the offense. Form an island with your body, keep close to the ground and keep your feet digging.

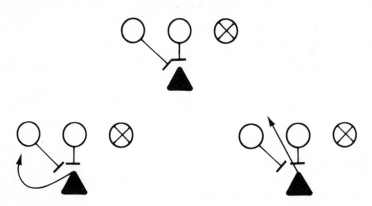

Three-on-One Block

This wedge block is used to gain short yardage near the goal line. It is difficult to overcome because you have three men blocking on you. Keep close to the ground in order not to offer a blocking surface to the offensive men and keep your feet digging.

Trap Block

This block is used basically on aggressive players, with either a scrape block or influence block being set up to allow the defender to cross the line of scrimmage. The off-side offensive lineman pulls behind his line and blocks square from the side. The key to this block is to recognize, when you feel no pressure, that something is wrong. Check to the inside first while keeping your shoulders square to the line of scrimmage in leverage position to defeat the trapper and drive the ball carrier away from his intended hole in the line.

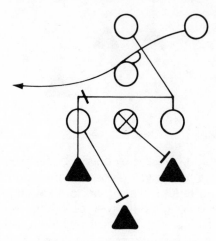

Influence Block

This is another type of block used on an aggressive player to make him commit himself at the line of scrimmage, but this time to put him out of position with his own momentum. Usually a trap or isolation block follows the influence block. To protect against this read your key and never start guessing. Look for any unusual style of play the defenders don't normally use and keep your eyes open for the trap.

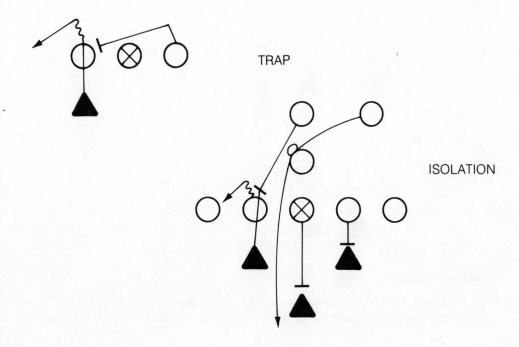

TRAP

ISOLATION

Scrape Block

This is a touch-and-go block usually used when you are not the primary target. The offensive man tries to tie you up just long enough for you to read him as a block, and then he goes for his primary block. You should consider this as a one-on-one block, and if you find that you are out of the play, tie up the blocker and don't let him finish his assignment.

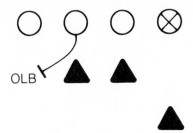

Slam, Fold, or Cross Block

These blocks are intended to give the blocker a better blocking angle on you. The offensive lineman playing over you gives you an influence block or goes to another assignment as you react while a man to either side of you makes the block. This gives him a good angle on you since he isn't coming in straight on, and he can hit you either high or low. The best way to protect yourself is to keep yourself in a leverage position, be aggressive, and use your defensive weapons.

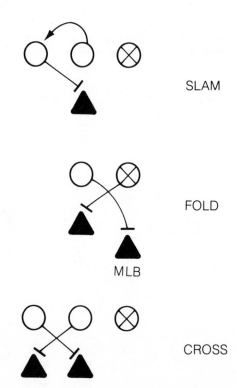

Crackback Block

This block can be dangerous unless your teammates help you to detect it. It is usually applied to the defensive end or linebacker. This block gives the offense outside running area, as the wide receiver or offensive ends come down and block in on the defense. The defensive halfback can be most instrumental in defeating this block by simply yelling, *"Crackback!"* This allows the defensive end or linebacker to be ready for the block and force the play back inside.

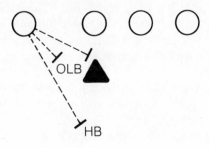

Pass Blocking

This type of block is the most obvious to the defensive lineman. Once pass protection forms and the quarterback sets up or rolls out, the play is obvious. You should make an all-out rush, stay in your lane, and break through the offensive line's protection. The first man through should be the sure tackler, while the others following put their hands in the air to obstruct the quarterback's vision. The defensive line and linebackers have blitzing and stunting to confuse the offense, and each individual can develop his own techniques to defeat pass protection. But the main goal is to put a heavy rush on the passes.

The pass rush should be a coordinated attack on the offense with defensive lineman, linebackers, and defensive backs. Each defender carrying out his responsibility protecting his territory and making the quarterback and receivers do things they do not like to do, throwing off time, throwing high or low, running a different pass pattern, or not completing one.

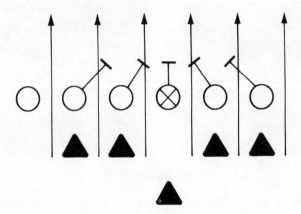

Defensive Skills

The leverage position is the basis for defensive play. You must never let yourself be caught in a vulnerable position. You leave yourself wide open to the offensive blocker by standing straight up, or lying on the ground and not snapping up. By not using your defensive weapons or your eyes you cannot neutralize or defeat a block or be in a position to tackle. You must keep your feet under your body in a coiled position ready to move right, left, or straight ahead with authority while letting your hands and arms act as shields and weapons to protect your legs and upper body surface and grasp offenders. Your neck should always be

Leverage position

bowed back, with your head up acting as a swivel and your eyes scanning the field to lead you to the play.

Another must in defensive play is *piston action* (leg drive) with your feet, the movement of your feet in an up-and-down action with authority in a forward motion. This will defeat any second effort after initial contact on the offensive blocker or ball carrier after the snap of the ball. Once you have neutralized the offensive personnel, you must keep your feet digging against offensive body pressure. Piston action will not only defeat any second effort, but will help in your pass rush, and is a vital part of the leverage position. You must never stop your feet after the initial blast.

Tackling is one of the key skills in the game of football. No matter how much they up-date coaching, plays, routines, and equipment, the game will still come back to tackling and blocking.

Tackling is probably one of the most misunderstood techniques. People think it is a natural movement. It is, however, a skill that demands a great deal of practice. You have to stop a running body going away from you and at the same time bring it to the ground. So you must know what you are doing. Any way that you can bring a ball carrier down should be considered a tackle. But if you use the proper technique you can be a lot more effective, and it can be a lot easier on you.

To make a tackle you must be physically and mentally ready. You have to get off the mark while keeping yourself in the leverage position. And most important, you must have your neck bowed back at all times. If you ever let your neck drop and be tucked under you can break your neck or do serious damage to it. By keeping your head up you can keep yourself in visual contact with the ball carrier. After the initial hit you must pop your hip through while wrapping the ball carrier up with your arms and hands. At the same time you must have follow-through with piston-action leg drive to stop the ball carrier and drive him back while preventing any second effort by him.

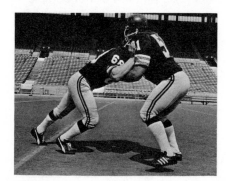

Leg piston action

If the tackle is made straight on, the *head tackle* is the best. Put the front part of your head gear and surface of your face mask right through the numbers or sternum of the ball carrier while popping the hips through and using the wrap-up technique with piston-action leg drive.

The *side tackle* should be made basically the same way. The head position is the only thing that changes. It should be in front of the ball carrier in the direction he is going, in the area of his numbers. This will help to neutralize the ball carrier's forward momentum.

Gang tackling consists of a group of defenders making a tackle at the same time on one ball carrier.

Pursuit angle is the best angle to the ball. The shortest distance between two points is not the proper pursuit angle. You must gauge your speed with the ball

Head tackle

carrier's speed, then try to force him to the sidelines. The sideline is the best tackler on the field.

Side tackle

Individual Techniques to Defeat and Neutralize Offensive Personnel:

Head Butt. Technique used on either the pass or run, and probably your most deadly weapon because you drive the top front part of your head gear at the offender's face.

Head butt

Hand slap

Slip under

Hand Slap. Technique used on either pass or run to throw the offender off balance. To perform this move you use an open hand and arm swing to the side of the offender's helmet. This usually turns the offender's head, and wherever the head goes, the body goes.

Slip Under. Technique used on the pass. This defensive move is used to outmaneuver the offender before he can get his blocking base. To perform this technique, dip your shoulder closest to the offender and try to slip under his arm and shoulder area.

Pull Over Technique used on the pass. This defensive move is used to outmaneuver the offender before he can get his blocking base. To perform this technique, grasp the offender and pull yourself past him with your outside hand and at the same time raise your inside arm over the offender's shoulder and head.

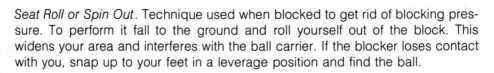

Pull over   Angle

Angle Left or Right Technique used on either pass or run to shoot the gap between defenders. To perform this technique, lead step in the direction you are going and never cross your feet. Get off on the snap and beat the offender through the gap.

Seat Roll or Spin Out. Technique used when blocked to get rid of blocking pressure. To perform it fall to the ground and roll yourself out of the block. This widens your area and interferes with the ball carrier. If the blocker loses contact with you, snap up to your feet in a leverage position and find the ball.

Jerk and Pull Down. Technique used on the pass to throw the offender off balance. To perform this technique, grasp the defender with your hands in an aggressive manner to try and drive him back. At the same time move to either side of the offender and pull or throw him away from you.

Seat roll   Jerk and pull down

Basic 43 Defense Alignment for Linebackers and Linemen

◯ ◯ ◯ ⊗ ◯ ◯ ◯

OSL   E   T   T   E   OSL

MLB

INDICATES:

◯   OFFENSIVE PLAYERS
⊗   CENTER
▲   DEFENSIVE PLAYERS
E   DEFENSIVE END
T   DEFENSIVE TACKLE
OSL   OUTSIDE LINEBACKER
LB   LINEBACKER
MLB   MIDDLE LINEBACKER

43 (OVERSHIFT)

◯ ◯ ◯ ⊗ ◯ ◯ ◯

OSL   E   MLB   T   T   OSL   E

Basic 54 Defense Alignment for Linebackers and Linemen

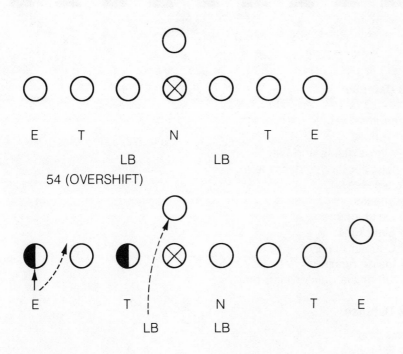

54 (OVERSHIFT)

6-5 Goal Line

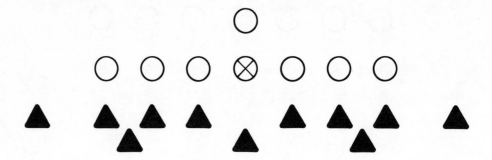

Gap 8 Goal Line

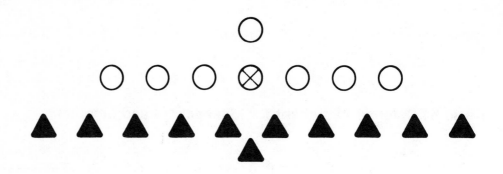

43 Defense

Strengths
— Outside
— Allows stunts and blitz
— four deep pass defenders
Weaknesses
— Sneaks
— Quick openers
— Slant runs
— Counter plays
— Inside running
— Off tackle quick hitting plays

54 Defense

Strengths
— Off tackle
— Rotation of backs
— Monster man effect for blitz
— Rollout pass play action
Weaknesses
— Inside running
— Cross blocking
— Turn out blocks
— Deep coverage

— Power sweeps
— Traps
— Reverse
— End around

DEFENSIVE TACKLE'S PLAY FOR THE 43 DEFENCE
Defensive Tackle Characteristics

1. Agressiveness

2. Ability to stay on feet

3. Good tackling and hitting

4. Good agility, and the ability to key and react to each offensive situation

5. Hard, tough worker

6. Mental and physical strength

Stance

The three- or four-point stance, whichever the defensive tackle finds most comfortable and efficient, can be used. There are some basic differences between the three- and four-point stances used by defensive and offensive linemen. By comparing this section to the offensive section of this book, the differences will be clearly illustrated.

Three-Point Stance

The feet are usually shoulder-width apart and staggered with a heel-toe relationship. This varies slightly, depending upon which position is most comfortable to the player. The advantage of this foot relationship is that it offers the lineman the ability to lead step right or left without crossing his feet. The three-point stance is used with either the left or right hand down on the ground, while the free arm is either in a cocked position paralell to the down hand or placed on the knee or thigh area, again depending on which is most comfortable to the defender. The tail should be as high as the shoulders or higher, with the head up. Always use a tripod stance with the fingers flexed along the ground. This will allow the tackle to claw for traction, which cannot be achieved with a closed fist.

Three-point stance

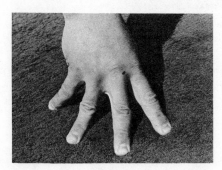

Hand

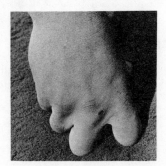

Knuckle

The tripod effect is the same as for sprinters leaving their mark; in fact, the sprinter and the lineman getting off the mark on the snap of the ball are in the same situation. When starting from this position, the defensive lineman drives with his up foot and steps with his back foot. To move into a running position quickly bring the back foot up paralell to the lead foot to obtain leverage position. This step must be taken automatically. Otherwise, with a step that is too long, the tackler will be prone to a block, or will lose the flow of play.

The three-point stance enables the tackle to find the play more quickly, because he isn't tied down with an extra hand on the ground, as with the four-point stance. But it can also be a hindrance unless the tackle stays low in leverage position until the offensive lineman is neutralized.

Four-Point Stance

This stance has the same basic foundation as the three-point stance. The only difference is that both hands are on the ground and are as wide or a little wider apart than the feet with the weight slightly shifted to the rear. Defenders like this stance because it enables them to move to the right or the left with basically the same motion. Also, the four-point stance enables you to stay lower and in a better leverage position than the three-point stance because both hands are on the ground. The four-point stance can give you problems if you cannot snap up to find the flow of play after the offensive lineman has made contact. The four-point stance is the basic goal line and short yardage stance. In this stance you are in more of a "cocked position" than in the three-point stance, with your head and shoulders closer to the ground, arms bent, and rear up.

This stance will give you a better penetration power and drive and at the same time will not give the offensive lineman a great amount of blocking surface or a good blocking angle.

Four-point stance

Tackle Alignment

Normally line up nose-to-nose over the offensive guard playing across from you. The tackles' alignment will vary at times according to the splits of the offensive line.

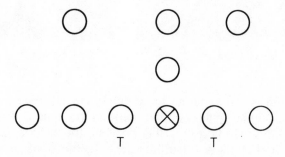

Responsibility

You are responsible for the offensive gaps between the guard and center inside, and the guard and tackle outside. You can never be driven back off the line of scrimmage, never be cut off by the center, never turn out by the guard, never let the guard inside on the middle linebacker. You must stop the middle trap and draws. At the goal line you must seal your area off and try to make the play.

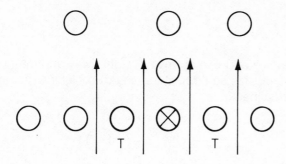

Pass

Pocket Pass. Free yourself from the offensive blocker and stay in your pass rush lane while checking for backs sneaking out of the backfield through your area on the draw or quarterback sneak. You must force the quarterback out of his pocket so the defensive rush can harass or pin him down.

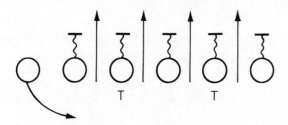

Rollout Pass. Free yourself from the offensive blocker. Take a proper pursuit angle. Check for cutback run and harass the quarterback.

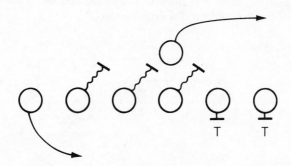

Keys. Movement on movement of the ball.
The tackle's line of vision should take in the guard, center, and tackle area.

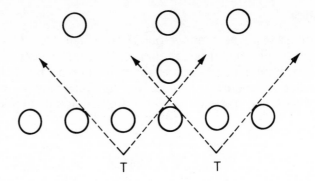

If the offensive tackle and center drive straight away and the guard blocks you straight ahead, neutralize and defeat the guard. Look for a quarterback sneak or handoff to either halfback.

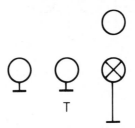

If double teamed by the guard and tackle, defeat the guard (post man) or the tackle (driver). Split, spin out, or form an island by bracing yourself close to the ground and keeping your legs driving. Never give up ground; you will cut off your linebackers if you do.

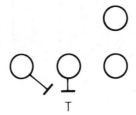

If guard pulls across your face to the outside and tackle slam blocks on you, meet pressure and keep shoulder square while moving down the line. If caught to far inside, spin against the pressure and pursue the ball. There are many combinations of this block that the offense use.

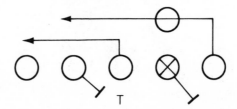

If the guard influences out and the tackle releases behind, check inside for the trap while keeping your shoulders square in a leverage position. Defeat the trapper and form an island, making the runner change his running hole.

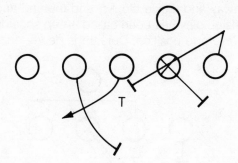

If the guard blocks you and the tackle pulls behind him, play through the guard's head and work to the inside.

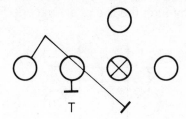

If the guard goes inside and no lineman blocks on you, be ready for the isolation block from the back.

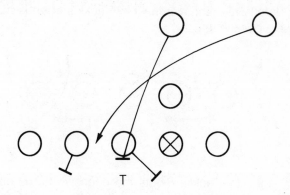

If linemen release downfield, the direction of their release will normally tell you the direction of the ball. Hit the man releasing in front of you and slide along the line of scrimmage towards the play. Do not penetrate into the backfield. After the runner has established himself pursue at an intercept angle. Make sure there is no cutback. Do not follow your own teammates.

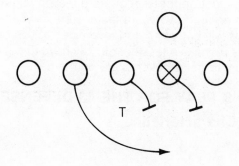

If the guard pulls away and tackle blocks, and the end and center use a cutoff block on you, an offside play has been called. Keep shoulders square to the line of scrimmage in a leverage position. Defeat the center and pursue the ball.

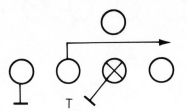

When offensive linemen set up for pass protection, rush while fighting toward passer. Check the halfback to your side for draws and screens. Hold up any back that tries to slip through the line of scrimmage for a pass.

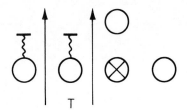

Stunt

The stunt is a defensive maneuver in which tackles or ends rush hard to penetrate the offensive backfield.

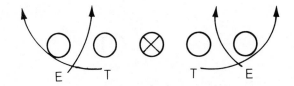

In the tackle's stunt, the tackle shoots the offensive tackle-end gap, while the end follows the tackle's play by shooting the offensive tackle-guard gap. The tackle wants to draw the offensive tackle and guard's block so the end will have a free path to the offensive backfield. Defensive stunting makes the offensive line more cautious to their blocking schemes and takes away some of their aggressiveness and confidence.

Aid in Stunting

Shift your weight to the foot opposite from the direction you are going. This will lighten up your lead step and give you a faster start for your stunt. Never cross your feet, because this will put you out of leverage position and you will not be able to take on a block or make a tackle. You may have to get deeper off the line of scrimmage in a stunt to get a better angle on the ball.

DEFENSIVE END'S PLAY FOR THE 43 DEFENSE

Defensive End's Characteristics

1. Agressiveness

2. Ability to stay on his feet

3. Good tackling and hitting

4. Good agility and ability to key and react to each offensive situation

5. Be a hard, tough worker

6. Quickness and strength

7. Ability to cover on a pass receiver

Alignment

Normally line up with your inside knee splitting the center of the offensive tackle. The end's alignment will vary according to the splits of the lineman and the offensive formation.

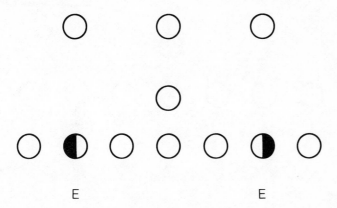

Responsibility

Run. You are responsible for the offensive gaps between the outside shoulder of the tackle and the outside shoulder of the end. You should never be driven back off the line of scrimmage, turned out by the tackle, turned in by the tackle, or be trapped. You must stop the off-tackle play and also check the counter reverse and then chase. On the goal line seal your area off and try to make the play.

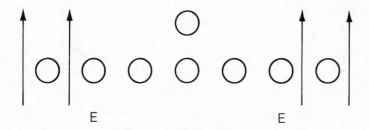

Pocket Pass. Free yourself from the offensive blocker and rush in your lane. You cannot get caught inside, you must contain rush outside, and never let the football get to the outside of you. When this happens the quarterback can set up again and become a "mad dog" passer, which is the most dangerous, because then he is a threat as both a passer and a runner. The ends are the sides of the cup on the pass rush. They must keep the quarterback bottled up so the defensive rush can harass him or tie him up.

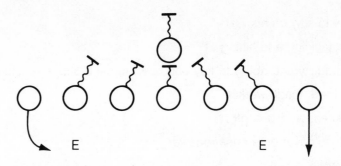

Rollout Pass. Free yourself from the offensive blocker, and get upfield on the ball. Hold up any back trying to sneak out of the backfield area. The end is responsible for any action coming back, as he is now the chaseman. Never get deeper than the ball.

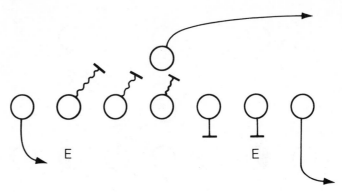

Keys. Movement on movement of the ball.
The end's line of vision should be inside of the nearest back. This will enable the end to have the back, running lane, and tackle in his vision. (See Diagram A.)

If there is no near back the end should have an imaginary line of vision the same as if there was a near back. (See Diagram B.)

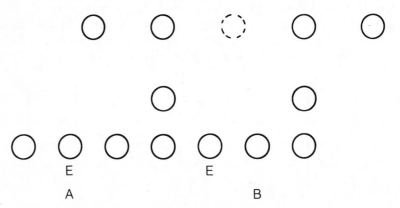

If tackle drives out straight, neutralize and defeat him.

If tackle uses a cut-off block on you after you drive across the line, expect an outside play. Work upfield and contain. Keep your shoulders square to line of scrimmage in a leverage position. Contain at all costs.

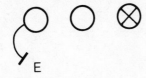

If tackle goes inside and wide receiver cracks back on you, neutralize and defeat him and contain the outside play.

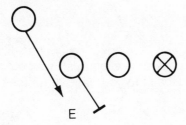

If double-teamed by the end and tackle, defeat tackle (postman) or end (driver). Split, spin out, or form an island by bracing yourself close to the ground and by keeping your legs driving. Never give up ground.

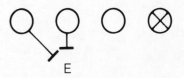

If the end goes inside and the halfback tries to block you, neutralize and defeat the back, contain or pursue the football.

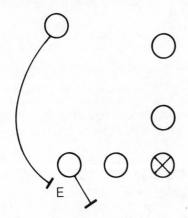

If the tackle pulls in front of you, play him and look for a toss to the near back.

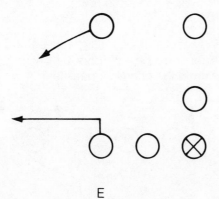

If the tackle pulls and there is no toss, check back for the running lane as the tackle pulling is to influence you out.

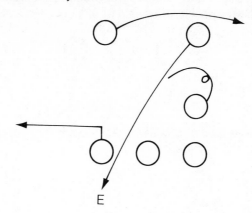

E

If the tackle sets up for pass protection, rush your lane. While fighting towards the passer, check the halfback to your side. If he tries to slip to the outside of you, contain the play.

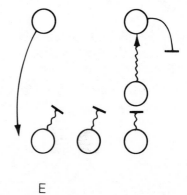

E

If the tackle releases inside, first check for a crackback block, then check inside for trap. While keeping your shoulders square in a leverage position, defeat the trapper, form an island and make the runner change his running hole.

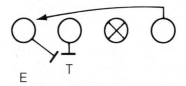

E   T

Stunt

In the end's stunt, the end shoots the offensive tackle-guard gap while the tackle follows. The end wants to draw the offensive tackle and guard block so the tackle will have a free path to the offensive backfield.

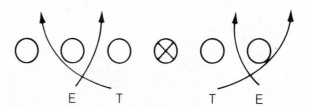

E   T   T   E

LINEBACKER PLAY FOR THE 43 DEFENSE

Linebacker's characteristics:

1. Agressiveness

2. Ability to stay on his feet

3. Good tackling and hitting

4. Ability to key and react to each offensive situation

5. Be a hard tough worker

6. Quickness and strength to blitz

7. Ability for good pass defense

8. Ability to be a defensive signal caller

OUTSIDE LINEBACKER

Stance

A staggered two-point stance with outside foot back. Your weight should be on the balls of your feet with your knees slightly bent, your arms should be in front of your body in a semi-flexed position ready to deliver a blow, and your hands should be ready to protect yourself.

Outside linebacker stance

Alignment

Your inside eye to the offensive player's outside eye. When offensive end is removed, line up over imaginary end and adjust to the offensive formation.

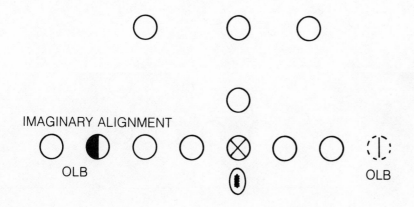

Responsibility

Run

1. Close offensive holes to the inside of you and try to make the play.

2. Make tackles.

3. Pursue when play is away from you.

Pass

1. If there is a tight end, deliver a blow to him for a short count so his pass pattern will be delayed, then drop back 10 to 15 yards to cover your territory in pass responsibility.

2. Never let any receiver cross in front of you free without delivering a blow to him.

3. Try to keep a 3-yard cushion on all pass receivers.

4. Always support on all screens and draws.

Keys

Look through the offensive end's head or through your guard and tackle to the quarterback area. If the end blocks down, close the hole and keep the area tight between you and the defensive end. Be prepared for either guard (1), tackle (2), or back (3) to block on you. Meet the blocker with feet perpendicular to the line of scrimmage and neutralize him.

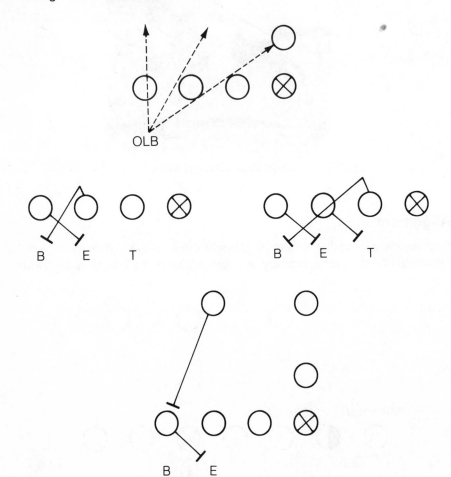

If the end blocks straight out at you set yourself in a leverage position and do not work to one side or the other. Force the end backwards and be able to meet a block from either the guard or the back, and find the ball carrier.

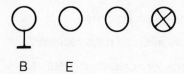

B   E

If the end releases outside, make sure he doesn't block you inside. Establish a pass defense and move to your area of responsibility.

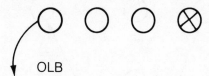

OLB

If the split end is to your side, key through the guard-tackle area to the quarter-back. React to your keys and check the split end for a crackback block on your second step.

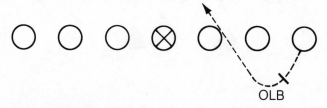

OLB

MIDDLE LINEBACKER

Stance

A two-point stance with feet shoulder-width apart, knees flexed, hips tucked, and back straight with head up. Your arms should be in front of your body in a semiflexed position ready to deliver a blow, and your hands should be ready to protect yourself. You must be able to move right, left, back, or forward with equal ability.

Alignment

Nose-to-nose with the offensive center. Your depth should be 5 to 6 yards from the line of scrimmage to read keys and move to the ball.

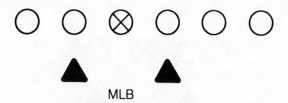

MLB

Responsibility

Run

1. Protect area over offensive center.

2. Play either side and pursue to make the tackle along the line of scrimmage.

Pass

1. On pass action, drop 10 to 15 yards into the middle area.

2. Never let any receiver cross in front of you without delivering a blow to him.

3. Watch for receivers coming into your area.

4. Try to keep a 3-yard cushion on all pass receivers.

5. Always support and check for screens and draws.

Keys. Center, guard triangle to the ball.

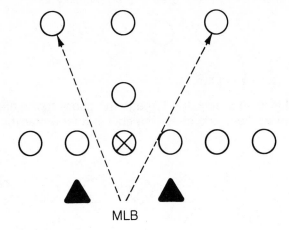

Both guards and center drive straight ahead. Meet the center nose-to-nose. Do not play either side. React to the play and find the ball.

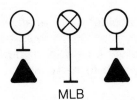

Center blocks back and guard blocks you while the other guard pulls. Meet the guard blocking you and play through his head or opposite shoulder, then react to the flow.

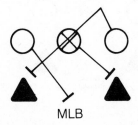

Guard pulls and center blocks out on you. Play through his head and work your way down the line with the pulling guards. Stay behind the ball and look for a cutback.

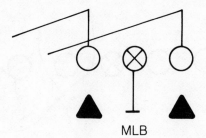

Center and two guards set in pass protection. Check for the draw on your way to pass responsibility. Key and move to your area of responsibility.

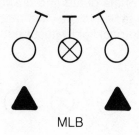

Pass Zone Areas

The blitz is a defensive maneuver in which the linebacker or linebackers rush hard to penetrate the offensive backfield.

PASS ZONE AREAS

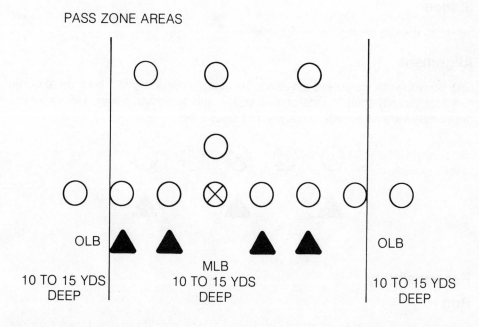

Blitz (A) Outside Linebackers

In the "A" blitz, the outside linebacker shoots the guard-center gap. The tackle angles to the outside shoulder of the guard to draw his block. The end does the same with the tackle.

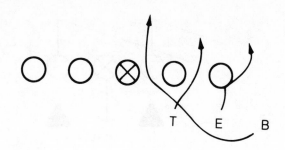

Blitz (B) Middle Linebacker

In the "B" blitz, the middle linebacker shoots the guard-tackle gap. The tackle angles to the inside shoulder of the guard and draws his block. The end angles to the outside shoulder of the tackle to draw his block, thereby freeing the middle linebacker to penetrate the backfield without getting blocked.

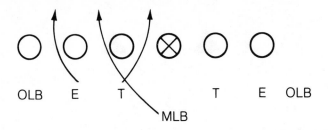

LINEBACKER'S PLAY FOR 54 DEFENSE

Stance

Same as middle linebacker in 43 defense.

Alignment

Line up with your inside eye on offensive guard's outside eye. The normal depth is a foot deeper than the defensive tackle and noseman's foot. (Alignment of depth may vary according to down and distance).

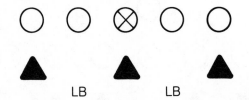

Responsibility

Run

Support on all plays from end to end, and attack outside plays. Make sure you always keep shoulders square along the line of scrimmage in a leverage position and use the shuffle step for transportation. This will enable you to meet blockers and runners with authority.

Picket and Roll Out Pass. Rotate your body to the outside and look for the first danger man in the passing area (usually the end). At the same time know where the passer is. Your depth should be 10 to 15 yards, then square up. Never let the end cross in front f you and always check backside for receivers entering your area. The two musts to pass defense are to read the pass quickly and get depth quickly.

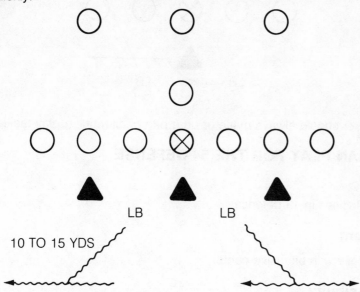

Keys-Guard to Halfback. At the snap of the ball and movement of the guard's head, take a slight jab step with the inside leg toward guard and keep the outside leg back and bent. The technique will always let you play the run first, pass second.

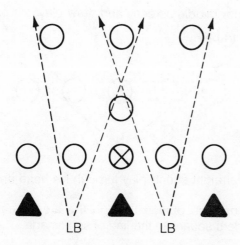

Play action toward you. You are responsible for the outside hole of the guard to your side.

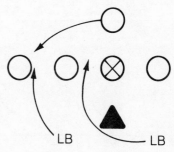

Play action away from you. You are responsible for off side guard and center hole. Shuffle down the line of scrimmage and stay one yard behind the ball carrier waiting for him to turn upfield.

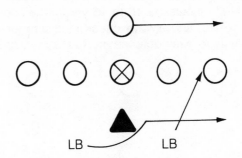

A linebacker should always make or be a part of all running play tackles.

NOSEMAN PLAY FOR THE 54 DEFENSE

Stance

Same as tackles in 43 defense.

Alignment

Nose-to-nose with offensive center.

Responsibility

Run

You are responsible for the area from tackle to tackle. Never let the center block you alone. Always make the offense use two men to block you.

Pass

You are responsible for middle screens and draw plays on passing situations.

Keys. Center's head to ball

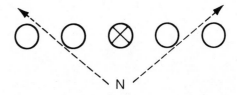

If center blocks you straight ahead play through his head and go to the ball.

If one or both guards pull, pursue through the area vacated by the pulling guards. Keep shoulders square to the line of scrimmage.

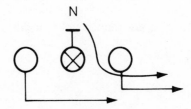

TACKLES PLAY FOR THE 53 DEFENSE

Stance

Same as tackles in 43 defense.

Alignment, Responsibility, Pass, Keys

Basically the same as the end's play in 43 defense.

ENDS PLAY FOR THE 53 DEFENSE

Stance

Same as outside linebacker's stance in the 43 defense.

Alignment

Same as outside linebacker's alignment in the 43 defense.

Responsibility

Run

Same as outside linebacker's play in the 43 defense.

Pass

No pass coverage on receivers, except possibly in blitzing or gaming situations. You must contain the passer at all times and make sure you get as deep as the ball and keep it to your inside.

Keys

Basically the same as outside linebacker's in the 43 defense.

THE DAY BEFORE THE GAME

The day before the game is as important as any practice day earlier in the week. This day lets your body recover physically. I follow the 48-hour rule, in which you begin to rest your legs and sharpen your mind 48 hours before the game. You can always think about the game, but you can only put in so many hours of physical exercise before your body becomes too tired to play. If you put too much physical stress on yourself, you will either lose your edge or your desire for the game. You must take care of your body.

In order to rest, the team usually has a 30 to 45 minute light workout without pads. Both offensive and defensive teams usually have calisthenics and work out their plays as a unit to avoid mental errors.

On the road, the team usually goes back to the hotel for a large meal and a meeting. Bed check is usually 11 o'clock.

DAY OF THE GAME

Players usually get taped in the morning, depending on game time. A pre-game meal usually follows. Some players can eat a large meal, some can't eat anything; it depends on the individual. Personally, I have a few pancakes with baked potatoes. This meal goes through your system well because it contains mostly carbohydrates. Some players prefer steaks, but since they are made up of protein, they take 5 to 6 hours to digest. Since they won't be digested until

Defensive equipment

after the game in this case, you have to play with them on your stomach. It's best to avoid them.

Before leaving for the stadium, we usually have a brief meeting and any special taping of knees and shoulders. I'm usually ready about an hour before game time.

Special teams are on the field 45 minutes before game time. Twenty minutes before the game the entire team is on the field for warm-ups, then back to the dressing room for last minute instructions and a moment of silence.

OFFENSIVE LINE PLAY

Tom Stillwagon,
Offensive Line Coach, Miami of Ohio

TOM STILLWAGON

Tom Stillwagon is offensive line coach at Miami University in Oxford, Ohio. He is a 1965 graduate of Miami and received his Master's Degree in Education from that institution the following year.

Some of the honors Stillwagon was accorded while at Miami, where he started for the Redskins each of his three varsity seasons, were: All Mid-American Conference, 1965; All-MAC Academic Team, 1964-65; Miami's Most Efficient Lineman, 1965; and honorable mention Academic All-American, 1964-65.

After graduation from Miami, he coached high school football for three years and one season at Hiram Scott College. From there he moved to the University of South Dakota as offensive line coach in 1971. In 1972, he became offensive line coach at Eastern Kentucky University for two years before coming back to Miami.

Stillwagon and his wife, Linda, have three children, Jeff (7), Brad (4), and Vince (3 months.)

FUNDAMENTALS OF OFFENSIVE LINE PLAY

The offensive line is composed of a center, two guards, two tackles, a tight end, and a split end.

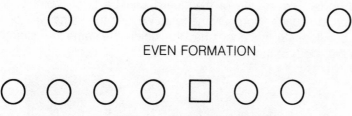

| SPLIT END | LEFT TACKLE | LEFT GUARD | CENTER | RIGHT GUARD | RIGHT TACKLE | TIGHT END |

The distance between each position varies according to which play is being run. On plays around the ends, the linemen will take narrow splits, normally 2 feet to 2 1/2 feet in distance, so that the defense will leave more running room on the outside. On plays on the inside the lineman will take larger splits, 3 feet to 3 1/2 feet, to make more running room on the inside.

Center

The center is the man who snaps the ball to the quarterback to start each play. He is normally found in the middle of the line on even formations, and on the right side or left side on unbalanced formations.

EVEN FORMATION

UNBALANCED FORMATION

On even formations there are an even number of people on the line on both sides of the center. On unbalanced formations there are more linemen on one side of the center than on the other. A center must be large enough to block defensive tackles and quick enough to pursue and block middle linebackers.

The stance of a center is a parallel toe-to-toe relationship. Feet are shoulder width apart and pointed straight up the field with weight on the balls of the feet. He must be able to step with either foot in the direction he is going.

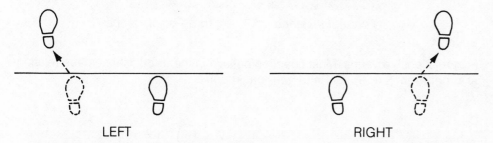

LEFT   RIGHT

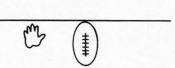

The ball will have the laces up for a right-handed quarterback, and down for a left-handed quarterback. In these positions, the ball will be received by the quarterback with the laces across his throwing hand in a position where he will not have to adjust the position of the ball in order to throw it. Either both hands or one hand can be placed on the football, depending on the individual center. If one hand is placed on the football, the other will be placed on the ground in a tripod position.

This type of hand position is very similar to a regular three-point offensive stance. Normally this hand position is used by guards or tackles who have been transferred to the center position.

When both hands are placed on the ball, the right hand will snap the ball and the left hand will be used as a guide hand. This is the best way to snap a football when the ball is wet and slippery. With both hands on the ball you have more control of the snap. The ball should be snapped in a lifting, and not jerked in a swinging motion.

The center's elbow should hit his inside thigh on the snap — this will indicate he is lifting the ball. The wrist is kept rigid on the snap, giving the ball a natural quarter turn when being received by the quarterback. The tail of the center is slightly higher than his head position. His legs are bent at the knees, ready to spring out f his stance when he snaps the ball.

The successful blocking center is one who learns to coordinate his feet movement at the same time as he moves the ball. This will enable him to get blocking angles on the defensive man.

A good center is very important in any successful offensive line.

GUARDS

The guards are located on either side of the center. They must be large enough to block defensive tackles and fast enough to pull and trap or lead sweeps around the ends. The stance of the guard can be three point or four point, depending on the coach. Normally the team will use the same type of stance for all lineman positions. Both stances have basically the same foot alignment. Feet are spread the width of the armpits.

Four-point stance   *Three-point stance*

Foot relationship varies. Most coaches believe in the traditional heel-toe relationship between your up foot and your back foot.

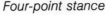

UP
FOOT

BACK
FOOT

The advantage of this foot relationship is the ability of the lineman to lead step right or left without crossing his feet. The lineman with this type of stance will push off from his up foot and step with his back foot.

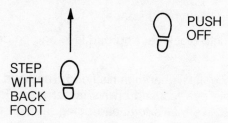

Once the guard has his feet properly aligned he assumes a squatting position with his elbows resting on his knees. This is very good position for pass blocking. Some teams will snap the ball while their linemen are in this position when they are going to pass.

To get into a three-point stance, the lineman reaches out with his hand on the side of his back foot.

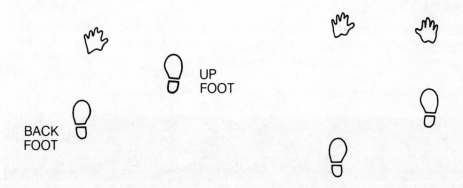

The arm on the side of his up foot is placed on his thigh. In a four-point stance, the lineman reaches out with both hands and places them in a tripod position. In comparing the two stances from the offensive point of view:

Four-Point Stance

STRENGTHS

1. Can stay low on firing out on block.

WEAKNESSES

1. Too much weight is forward, making it difficult to go right or left.

2. Difficult stance to set from on pass protection.

3. Difficult to pull to trap from this type of stance.

Three-Point Stance

STRENGTHS

1. Can move right or left easily.

2. Pulling is not difficult from this position.

3. Pass protection position is easier from this position because most of weight is on the balls of the feet.

WEAKNESSES

1. Tendency to relax in this type of stance.

2. Can fire out higher into block causing bad leverage on defensive man.

The guard's tail is slightly higher than his head. The head is cocked slightly in an up position with his eye focused on his target area. The target area for a down man is the offensive man's forehead going through the defensive man's chin. When blocking an up defensive man, the target is the numbers. The offensive man should have leverage when blocking a defensive man. This means that the defensive man is higher than the offensive man.

If the defensive man is under the offensive man, then the offensive man must thigh block him by driving his thighs like pistons into the defensive man in order to move him and create a hole for the offensive back. If a team wants to trap and have power sweeps, then they must have good guards on their offensive line.

TACKLES

The two remaining interior linemen inside the ends are the tackles. They have basically the same responsibility as the guards, but do not pull as much from their position. They are usually the largest linemen, because they block the largest defensive people. To have strong off tackle plays, the bread and butter of most offenses, the offense must get movement in this area.

Their stance is the same as the guards. The tackle normally blocks down linemen, but occasionally they will pull with the guards to lead power sweeps. If you intend to run this type of offense, then your tackles will have to perform the pulling technique.

To pull, the lineman must shift his weight away from the side of the pull. The purpose of this maneuver is to enable the tackle to take a short step in the direction he is pulling. At the same time as the short step, the lineman must pull his inside elbow back and keep it close to his body. He must point his toe in the direction he is going. At the same time the head and shoulders are snapped around in one continuous motion. The next step is a regular step. Stay low and be ready to block a defensive person at any time during the pull.

The pull

The tackle position is a key position for a strong running game. He, along with the guards, must control the largest defensive people.

ENDS

The ends are found on the line of scrimmage and are on the outside of the line. There is usually, in today's type of football, a tight end and a split end. The split end is usually a pass receiver first and a blocker second. The tight end is just the opposite — receiver second and blocker first. The split end is normally split from 5 to 15 yards from the tackle.

The stance of the split end is a two-point or standing type, in which the end has his hands on his hips looking in to the quarterback, or a three-point stance. The two-point stance is best to enable the end to see which coverage he will be facing, as well as seeing the snap of the football.

The tight end lines up next to the tackle with a 3 to 4 foot split. He is normally large and tall and is capable of running with good speed. He must be strong enough to block outside linebackers. The split end does not have to be big but should have very good speed, quickness, and be able to catch the football.

Both ends should be good downfield blockers. In performing this block the offensive end must keep his eyes on the target — the defensive man. Do not look for the ball carrier — he will find you. The defensive man's eyes, face and reactions will tell you when there is action behind you. Timing is one of the keys to good downfield blocking — not too soon or not too late. When you attack the man you want to block, try to run through him. A wide base with short steps will help you keep from getting faked. Keep your head up. The end should not throw a block if he is in a clip position — don't clip. The offensive ends are very important in both the running and passing games. With poor ends you severely limit your offense.

BASIC EXECUTION OF BLOCKING TECHNIQUES OF OFFENSIVE LINEMEN

The offense is made up of plays that involve each player doing a specific task to move the football forward. Specific tasks consist of blocking schemes. The technique involved in each blocking scheme will be discussed in this section.

One-On-One Block

Purpose: To block a man at the point of attack when you are moving the defender in either direction to create a hole.

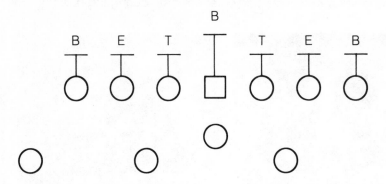

This block is the toughest to master. The head-on block seems simple but takes a great deal of practice to accomplish. The simplest way to teach this block is to break it down into different segments. First, you must learn the stances which we discussed in the last section. Second, the lineman must know how to position himself properly when he faces his block.

The breakdown of this body position is:

1. Head up and in the numbers.

2. Back arched.

3. Forearms up and in front of the offensive man. This is called the blocking surface and keeps the defensive man from sliding off the block. The blocking surface is the distance between the elbows. The shorter the distance between the elbows, the smaller the blocking surface.

4. Legs bent and flexed.

5. Feet shoulder width apart and straight up field, with weight on balls of feet.

One-on-one block

After the offensive man has assumed and felt what it's like to be in this position, he now moves with short choppy steps in the direction of defensive man.

Third, the offensive man must position himself properly when he is one step from the defensive man he is going to block. He will be low with his head in an up position and eyes focused on the target area. Next, he has his forearms located slightly behind his hips in a ready position. Now he must take a step toward the man being blocked and coordinate his forearms coming forward to form a blocking surface, while at the same time his head makes contact against his target, the defensive man's numbers. This puts him back into contact position and he again drives the man backwards.

Fourth, he now assumes his stance and fires out and blocks the man. He has now felt and seen each position he should be in when blocking one-on-one.

Two-On-One Block

Purpose: To assure movement of the defensive man away from the one of attack in a specific direction.

This block can be made anywhere along the line of scrimmage by two offensive people blocking one defensive man. The technique involved in performing this block takes coordination of the two blockers working as one. The man who blocks the defensive man head-on is called the *post man.* He performs the one-on-one technique; in fact, he should be coached so that he will block the man by himself until he feels pressure from the side by the other offensive man who is helping him.

The man who is blocking from the side is called the *drive man.* On the snap he takes a step with the foot to the side of the defensive man and aims his head towards the hip area of the defender, making contact with the shoulder farther on the side of the post man. The head slides from the hip to behind the defensive man. A wide foot base should be maintained throughout the block by the drive man.

When the post man feels the pressure from the outside, he swings his tail to the drive man. They are now working together, closing the area between them. The defensive man must not split the post and drive man in this block. They then drive the man being blocked at a 45-degree angle away from where the ball is being carried.

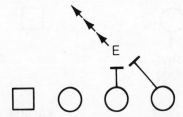

This is relatively an easy block when the defensive man is firing straight out into the post man. There must be an adjustment when the defensive man angles towards or away from the two-on-one block.

A. Angles towards Block

The adjustment is made by both the post and drive man. The post man must position his head in the middle of the defensive man and the drive man's head will be in front of the man instead of behind. They will stay in front and let the man take himself out of the play by creating a hole in that area of the defense.

B. Angles away from Block

The post man must block the man over him by himself, driving the man in the direction away from the two-on-one block. The drive man is not needed when the defensive man makes this maneuver, so he now continues ahead, picking up the linebacker in the area.

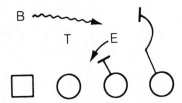

Three-On-One Block

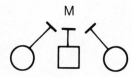

Purpose: To converge three blockers on one to assure movement backwards in that area.

This is a wedge blocking scheme when short yardage is needed. *The point of attack* is the area where three linemen work shoulder-to-shoulder to block on one man. The lineman should shorten their splits to a 1 1/2 feet on this block.

Fold Block

Purpose: To enable linemen to get better blocking angles on defensive linebackers.

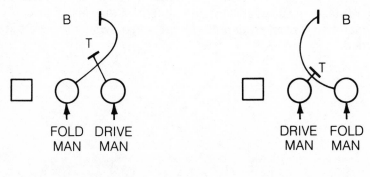

GUARD FOLD BLOCK   TACKLE FOLD BLOCK

This block involves two linemen exchanging areas of blocking responsibility. The man who is blocking down is called the *drive man* and performs basically the technique involved in the two-on-one block, except that his head goes in front of the man. The man stepping around is called the *fold man.* His first move is to replace the near foot position taken by the drive man from his stance.

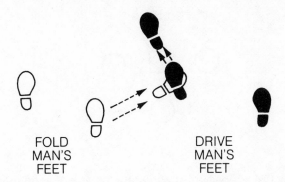

FOLD MAN'S FEET

DRIVE MAN'S FEET

At the same time as this step is being taken, the hand on the side of the step reaches and is placed on the tail of drive man, which helps in pulling himself around the man and also keeps his shoulders parallel to the *line of scrimmage.* The line split should be narrowed down to help in this block. The fold man should be ready to block as soon as he clears the drive man.

Fold block

Cut-Off Block

Purpose: To lead the man toward the play area and cut off his pursuit.

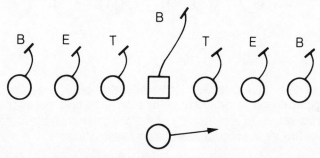

This block is executed by leading the man to the play side and anticipating where he will be when you reach that point.

Drive your shoulder into the side of defensive man with your head between him and the ball carrier. Block the man upfield or stay with him and run him past the ball carrier. If your block goes away from you, continue towards the point of attack and block the first defensive man you see in the area.

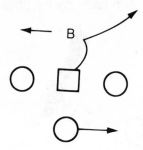

Trap Block

Purpose: To allow the opposition to penetrate the line of scrimmage, making the defender think he can execute the tackle, while pulling a man from another position to block him.

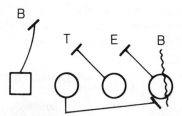

The man trapping takes a short step in the direction of the block, replacing the foot of the man next to him. The toe is pointed in the block direction. On this step the trapper pulls his elbow to the side of the trap, and keeps it in close to his body. This helps turn his body. The trapper must be ready to block at any moment of the play. He has to be ready to pick up blitzing linebackers that might penetrate the backfield before he has reached the trap area.

Influence Block

Purpose: To give a false key to the defensive man.

These blocks give false direction to the offensive play. They can be misleading when the guards pull in one direction, then turn and go in the other. These blocks can be set up to look like a pass block, then trap the defensive man. These blocks are very good against strong keying teams.

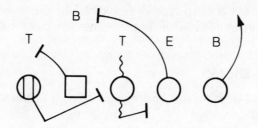

Scrape Block

Purpose: To stop the *initial* charge of the defense man, and then go to another block.

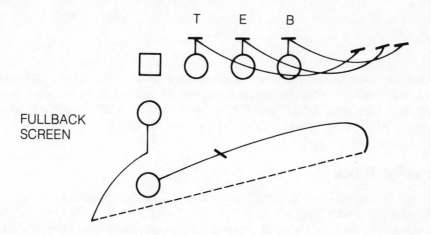

FULLBACK
SCREEN

These blocks are used primarily in fullback and quick screens.

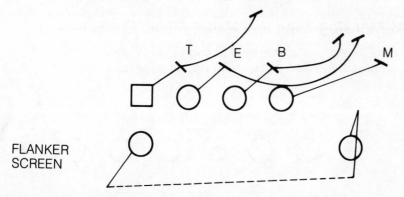

FLANKER
SCREEN

The scrape block involves delivering a forearm and then releasing from the man and heading towards the area you are going to block.

Slam Block

Purpose: To stop a pass rush or pursuit from a defensive man.

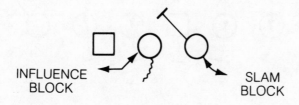

INFLUENCE
BLOCK

SLAM
BLOCK

The slam block is a chop type of block into the defensive man's legs. Normally one lineman influences while another lineman blocks down on the defensive man.

Crackback Block

Purpose: Used by a flanker or split end coming inside to block a linebacker or defensive end.

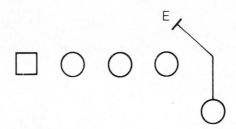

The outside man should keep his stance the same as on all other plays. Open with inside foot — step and go. Your target area is the hip. Drive head across defender's path and hit to knock him down. If you don't knock him down, scramble on all fours. Never clip; it is not only a penalty but sometimes causes very serious knee injuries.

Scramble Block

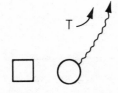

Purpose: To get into the defensive man's legs, causing him difficulty in pursuing to the point of attack.
Fire out and throw your hands and arms out past the defensive man, bridge up and scramble downfield on the hands and feet. This block doesn't move people but ties them up, giving the ball carrier time to get past the area.

Pass Blocking-Zone and Man-For-Man Protection

Purpose: To give the quarterback enough time to pass the ball to his receivers. In zone pass protection, each man protects an area.

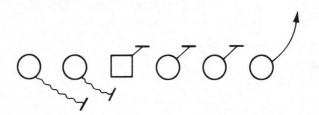

In man-for-man pass protection, each offender takes a specific defender.

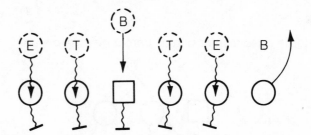

The technique for pass blocking is different than that for the running game. In the running game you go after people and are over-aggressive, while in the passing game you are more patient and wait for the defensive man to come to you. In the passing game, having enough time to throw the ball is the most important factor. The longer the defensive man takes in getting to the passer, the higher the chances of a completed pass.

The pass blocking set position is:

1. Head up, eyes on target.

2. Back in an arched position.

3. Tail low.

4. Elbows in close to the body.

5. Hands fisted.

6. Knees bent.

7. Feet pointed straight up the field and moving with short choppy steps.

Pass blocking set position

From this position the offensive man prepares himself to block the defensive man by using his forearms as battering rams, and not over-extending his weight forward. Once you become over-extended, you lose control of your body, and the defensive man can step around you or pull you out of his way. You must set back and maintain body control, and keep your tail facing the quarterback, so the defensive man works through you.

The "don'ts" in pass protection are:

1. Don't let the defensive man head you up.

2. Don't let the defensive man get his hands on you.

3. Don't give ground unless the man is attacking you.

4. Don't stop chopping your feet.

5. Don't over-commit.

6. Don't get your feet close together.

7. Don't lose your man immediately.

8. Don't straighten up your legs — keep them bent.

You must know where the passer is going to be when passing the ball in order to get in the proper position to block the defensive man.

CENTER SPECIALTY SKILLS

The center specialty skills include the snaps for punts, extra points, and field goals. They are skills that must be developed through coaching and practice. The center must be able to throw a football just as the quarterback does when throwing to a receiver. If he cannot throw a football correctly, then he must be taught.

To throw a football grip it with the index finger 1 to 1 1/2 inches from the end of the ball. The third finger should be in the second lace area. The grip should be adjusted according to the size of the hand. You should be able to get the fingers of the other hand between the fingers of the throwing hand. Bring the ball to a throwing position by leading the arm back with the hand. Lead with the elbow and lock the wrist when throwing the ball, and make sure to follow through.

Once the fundamentals of throwing the ball have been learned, the centre can practice throwing it back and forth with the coach, at a distance of 15 yards, progressively throwing it harder each time. He can turn his back to the coach and pass it between his legs, using the same passing motion.

This drill gives the centre an idea of what he will have to do when he snaps the ball. But he will not have much control over the ball when throwing in this manner. To have control over the pass, he must use his other hand as a guide hand. The center should now get into his snapping stance. His stance will have a wider base than a normal stance with his weight on the heels of his feet. This will help keep his tail down and bend his legs, which is important in keeping the ball low on the snap.

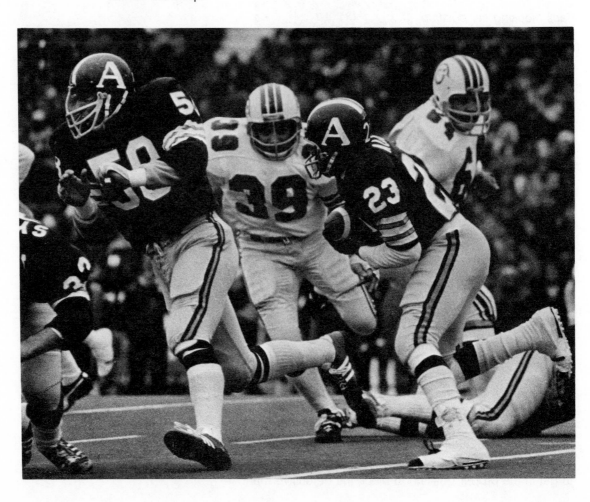

To assume the correct position of the hands when snapping, set the ball with strings touching the ground and grip the ball. The other hand is the guide and is placed on top of the ball with the second finger going straight down the seam of the ball. There is no weight placed on the ball by the guide hand; its only purpose is to control the ball.

The center should not have much weight on the ball; in fact, he should be able to let go of the ball with his hands and still maintain his stance without falling flat on his face.

When looking under his legs from his stance, he should see only the punter from the waist down. If he sees the whole punter, then he has not reached out far enough with the ball. On the snap, the passing hand and guide hand must move together in one action, in a straight backward direction — the hands should not turn right or left. The ball will move backwards, almost touching the ground throughout the snap. The ball should have a bullet-like spiral on it, aimed at the waist of the punter. The speed of the snap on the punt is very important and should be .7 or .8 seconds when the punter is 13 yards away, and .8 to .9 at 15 yards. The total time of the snap and punt should not exceed 2.1 seconds.

After the release of the ball from the center's hands on the punt snap, the forearms should have a lifting motion to help protect the center and bring his head up. The center should never look back after snapping the ball to see if the snap was a good one. There is nothing he can do to improve the snap once the ball has left his hands, and he can also be blocked while looking backwards, which can result in an injury.

The snap on the extra points and field goals are shorter snaps. Normally the snap will be about 7 yards to the holder. The stance for extra points is basically the same as discussed previously. The snap is a little softer than for the punt so that the holder can catch the ball easily. The center aims for the holder's hands, which will mean that the snap has to be lower than for the punt. The center must therefore keep his tail lower for this type of snap. The snap should reach the holder's hands in .4 to .5 seconds, and the kick should take .6 to .8, making the total time 1.0 to 1.3 seconds for the complete kicking cycle.

It is very important that the center learn to make a perfect snap every time, because a snap that is too high or low will result in the kicker having to rush the kick, even though the protection is good.

RUNNING
AND PASS RECEIVING
Jim Young, British Columbia Lions

JIM YOUNG

Jim Young is an offensive football player with the B.C. Lions in the Canadian Football League; he has played running back, tight end and both wide receiver positions for the Lions and is best known as a pass receiver and downfield blocker.

Upon graduation from Queens University in 1965 with a Bachelor of Arts degree in Psychology, Jim was drafted number one in the country by Toronto Argonauts but chose to sign with the Minnesota Vikings of the N.F.L.

After two years with the Vikings, the B.C. Lions traded players to Toronto for his rights and QB Joe Kapp to Minnesota for his contract. He has played with B.C. since 1967.

Some honors bestowed on Young are as follows: western representative as outstanding Canadian player 1969; outstanding Canadian 1970, 1972; chosen to play in all five all-star games (only player to play for the all-stars in all five games).

Young currently ranks eighth in all time C.F.L. receiving records.

THE RUNNING GAME

Offensive football is based on control of the ball, hopefully taking it in for the score, but controlling it so that the opposition cannot score. A good running game is the best weapon in doing this. The ball is protected and, except for a fumble, the opposition has little chance to take it away.

When the running game is going well, it sets up the pass, as the defensive backs begin creeping up to try to make the tackles sooner and therefore are not as pass-concious as usual; in this case a play pass, a pass designed to look to the other team just the same as the run it is based on, is the best pass to attempt, since the defensive backs may be fooled long enough to get the pass to a receiver before he can be covered.

Good coaches strive to have an offense that gains about the same yardage running and passing; this means that they run the ball more often than they pass, since usually the average gain per run is only half or less than the average gain per pass completed. Runs also use more time on the clock, as the clock continues to move after a run but is usually stopped after a pass until all the receivers are back to the huddle. This means that a team moving the ball on the ground uses up more of the time the opposition has for scoring and therefore helps the defensive team's effort.

Weather conditions affect the running game far less than the passing game and thus provide one more reason to stress the run. No matter what the conditions, a team that can move the ball along the ground for a score is far more secure than a team that bases its offense primarily on passing. Ball control and points on the board are the name of the game.

RUNNING

Running with the ball is the thing most backs like to do best, and is the basis for calling any back a running back. His job, when he is not blocking, is to run with the ball for yardage. In this section I will concentrate on running the ball from the line of scrimmage.

The running back can line up behind the line of scrimmage in several positions, which are shown below in two different running situations:

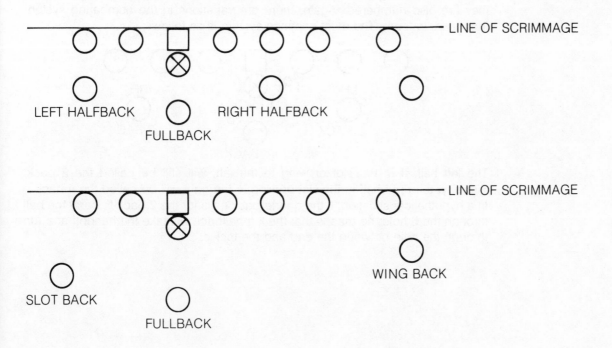

There are only three backs in the backfield at any one time, and the position of each is determined by which formation the quarterback calls in the huddle.

The alignment of these running backs, how they line up in relation to one another and to the linemen, is very important, since the timing of the plays depends on each player being in the right position. The following are the alignments of the running backs:

Left Halfback: 1' to 1½' in front of the fullback and 5' to the left of him, regardless of the line split.

Fullback: His heels should be 4½ yards from the ball. He should be directly behind the centre and the quarterback.

Right Halfback: 1' to 1½' in front of the fullback and 5' to the right of him, regardless of the line split.

Slotback: 1 yard wider and 1 yard deeper than the tackle on whose side he's playing. The slot back can play either left or right depending on which side the tight end lines up.

Wingback: 1 yard wider and 1 yard deeper than the tight end on the same side of the field as the tight end.

PLAYS

Hole Numbering

In order for the quarterback to tell a running back where to take the ball, all of the spaces between the linemen are numbered. Each team may have a slightly different system to number the holes, but the following system is most commonly used:

Back Numbering

In order for the backs to tell which of them is to carry the ball on any given play, they are also numbered. Again, there are variations in the numbering system from team to team. The most common system is as follows:

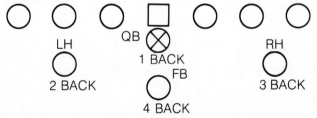

The left half, if in the slot or wing to the left, will still be called the 2 back. Similarly, the right half in the slot or wing to the right will be called the 4 back.

In a hypothetical situation, if the quarterback calls for the 2 back to carry the ball through the 6 hole, he means that the left halfback will take the handoff and run through the hole between the end and the tackle.

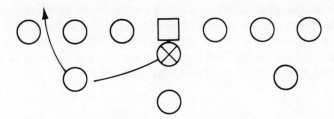

Series

The series called on a play tells the backs, especially those not running with the ball, which fakes or blocks they must carry out. On each series the backs generally go through the same motions whether or not they receive the ball. In this way several different plays that attack different points along the line look very similar to the defenders. The following examples show different series:

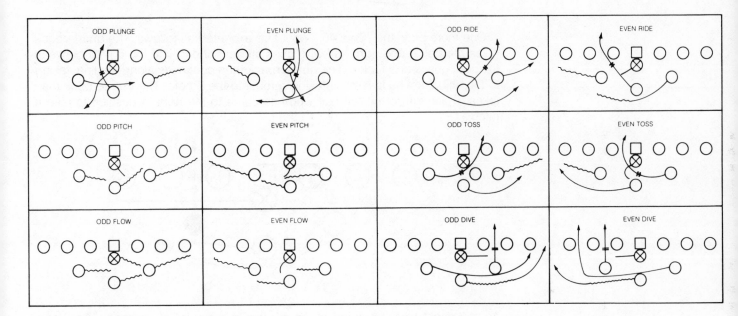

CALLED PLAY

Using what we have learned about the series, hole numbers, and back numbers, it is possible to call a play. For example, let's call a "Plunge 27." Looking back to the plunge series we see that the quarterback fakes to the fullback and hands the ball to the left halfback while the right halfback leads the blocking at the 7 hole between the right tackle and end. The heavy line indicates the ball:

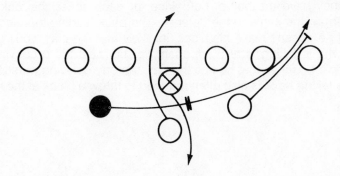

Another example of a called play could be the "Ride 36." On this play the left half leads the blocking, the quarterback hands the ball to the fullback on his way to the 6 hole between the left tackle and end, and the quarterback continues towards the left as if he still had the ball, then fakes a pitchout to the right half who has come to the left in position to take the pitch:

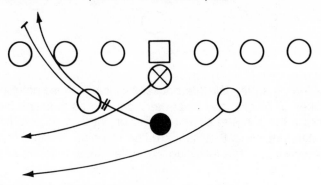

One more play, the "Dive 45," would be executed as follows. The quarterback gives the ball to the right half who goes straight ahead into the 5 hole between the right guard and tackle. The quarterback then continues along the line, faking to the fullback who is himself faking a run into the 7 hole. The quarterback then fakes a pitchout to the left half who has come to the right in position to take a pitch.

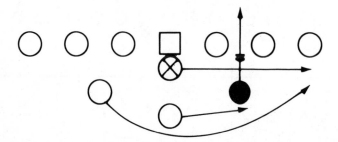

As you might imagine, each of these plays takes a lot of practice. The timing must be perfect: each player has to be in just the right position at the right time for the hand-offs and fakes.

For variations on these plays look back to the "Plunge 27." From the same series, and without changing the look of the defense very much, we can run the "Plunge 30," "Plunge 34," "Plunge 25," "Plunge 29," and "Plunge 19 Quarterback Keep." The same type of thing can be done for each series to make up an entire running playbook.

We must keep in mind at all times that each of the backs is important on every play, whether they have the ball or not, since for each series the look of the offense must remain the same to the defense. The back leading the blocking is important, for if he doesn't make his block, its likely that the play won't go very far. The back who is faking is also important, for he must try to convince the players at the hole he fakes that he has the ball, thereby delaying pursuit of the ball carrier. The faking back is also often required to throw a block at the hole he is faking.

TECHNIQUES

Stance

Backs begin all plays from the stance. It is basic to all running and passing plays, and must be practiced and become comfortable before maximum efficiency can be achieved. In the stance, feet should be shoulder-width apart, with one foot (the one on the side of the hand down) dropped slightly back, so that the toe is about even with the instep of the other foot. The hand that is down should be placed so that balance can be maintained without weight being placed on the hand. The neck should be arched with the head up and the line of the back paralell with the ground.

Runner's stance

Coaches may like slots and wings to face inward at about a 45-degree angle, but the basic stance for these players is still the same as for the other backs.

Taking the Handoff

Since there are two widely accepted ways of taking the hand-off from the quarterback, one should be chosen by the coach and practiced by the backs until they automatically take the ball that way.

The first method of taking the hand-off is with the inside arm (the one closest to the quarterback) across the chest about on a line with the armpits, and the outside arm forming a pocket underneath. The elbow of the arm is pressed against the side and the hand is open to prevent the ball from slipping through when handed by the quarterback.

The second accepted method of taking a hand-off has the player accepting the ball with both hands in the belly area. In this method the pocket for the ball is formed by the hands and the belly, and the stress must be put on waiting for the quarterback to place the ball in the pocket rather than having the back grab for it. The elbows are both at the sides with the hands open and relaxed. This method has been described as "like taking a loaf of bread."

There are a couple of hand-off drills that can be used to practice accepting the ball. Form two lines of players facing each other, with the first player in one line having the ball. He walks to the other line and hands the ball off to the first player there. The first player in this line then repeats the procedure, handing the ball to the first player across from him. Once a player has handed-off he goes to the back of the line, and will receive a hand-off when the ball comes back to him. The drill is over once each player has both handed-off and received a hand-off. Once the drill has been carried out at a walk a few times it can be speeded up, but stress must be placed on taking the hand-offs properly rather than on speed.

Another hand-off drill involves players pairing off. Have both players take turns at acting as quarterback and at running out of the stance. This drill is designed both to improve skill at taking hand-offs and in practicing running from the stance. Both the hand-off and the stance will soon begin to feel natural.

Faking

When a back runs into the defensive line on a fake run, the object is to make the defending players think that this back has the ball, and it will, if carried out properly, prevent them from reacting quickly to the actual ball carrier. It stands to reason that the faking back must do exactly the same things as if he did have the ball in order to deceive the defense. Thus the back forms the same pocket to receive the ball, and the quarterback either puts the ball in and takes it out again or puts an empty hand into the pocket. The back then runs hard into the line as if trying to gain yards. If not tackled on the fake, the back looks for someone to block.

Blocking

It has been acknowledged that the two most basic things in football are blocking and tackling. Both basics are related, the only real difference being that the blocker is not supposed to use his hands to push or grab the defender.

To block or tackle effectively all football players must lean to get their bodies into what we call the "hitting position" just before contact is made. Once in "hitting position" the player is able to deliver the most effective blow and have the best chance of maintaining balance to carry through with another blow if the defender recovers. The basic blocking position is shown below, feet about shoulder-width apart, knees bent, tail down, arms either down, slightly bent with the fists closed ready to club up around the ball carrier if tackling, or tucked up into the chest loosely if blocking, the neck arched or bowed to deliver the blow, and the eyes looking up at the numbers of the player to be hit.

Blocking position

The blow should be delivered with the whole body, the main power coming from the strong thigh muscles, and should be aimed at the number of the defender's sweater. The blow with the best results is delivered with the forehead right at the numbers with the head, then sliding off to one side or the other and the shoulder carrying on with the momentum right through the player. The legs should remain slightly bent, driving like pistons with short choppy steps, still shoulder-width apart to maintain the all-important balance. If the opponent does knock you down, an effective block can still be made by scrambling on all fours, or "crabbing," keeping your body between him and the ball carrier.

For the best position on the initial hit the head should slide so that it is between the opponent and the ball carrier and the blocker should remain on his feet, driving the player as long as possible.

Pass Blocking

The back delivers the initial blow to stop most of his momentum, stays on balance, backs off slightly (usually the hit will knock the blocker back slightly), gets back into the hitting position, and delivers another blow, always being careful to stay between the rusher and the quarterback. Of course, the defender will be trying to avoid these hits, so the blocker must always keep his eyes on the defender and keep his feet moving quickly with short choppy steps to be in position.

Drills that can help develop good blocking techniques are as follows:

1. The back lines up his stance in the backfield and another player lines up in the position of a defensive end or linebacker, holding a large dummy. On command the back starts out of the backfield to block the dummy. The player holding the dummy steps up slightly and gives the back resistance to the block. The back tries to drive the dummy back, maintaining good balance and hitting posture. So that the back knows which way to slide his head on the hit, the coach calls out which hole the ball carrier would be running into and the blocker tries to drive the dummy away from the hole. This drill must be done many times, with the coach pointing out mistakes, such as getting the feet too

close together and losing balance, or extending too far out of the hitting position and consequently having no drive left in the legs. Other mistakes, such as sliding the head to the wrong side and therefore blocking with the wrong shoulder, become apparent. Some players always want to hit with the same shoulder no matter where the play is going; other players duck their heads rather than keeping their necks arched and eyes up watching the opponent. These are bad techniques, for in a game situation it gives the opponent an opportunity to avoid the block, and could result in neck injuries.

2. The back lines up in position in his stance ready to step up slightly to pass block on command. A linebacker holding a small hand dummy lines up in his relative position and gives the command to pass rush. The back delivers the initial blow, tries to keep balance and delivers a second and then a third blow as in a game. Coaching points to watch for are good hitting positions, balance, quick footwork, getting back into hitting position for the second and third hits, and maintaining position between rushes and where the quarterback would be.

CARRYING THE BALL

Possession of the ball is one of the most important aspects of football, so once a back is handed the ball by the quarterback he must learn to protect it and not fumble. Quickly tuck the ball under one arm or the other, usually the side away from where the majority of the tacklers are coming from with the elbow down tight against the side to prevent the ball being pushed out from the rear, and the point of the ball held firmly between the thumb and first finger. In traffic, the other hand can be wrapped across the top of the ball for better protection.

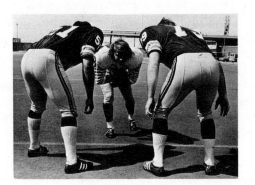

Carrying the ball

When running with the ball many of the same principles as those used in blocking are employed. Balance is all-important, since once the ball carrier is knocked down the play is over. The runner must run as close to the hitting position as possible, leaning slightly forward, legs bent for power and shoulder width apart for balance. Once hit he must use the same short choppy leg drive to try to rid himself of the tackler. If a tackler cannot be avoided, the ball carrier is much better off to deliver the blow himself in much the same way as a block, and then try to slide away from the tackler.

The arm not holding the ball can be used as a weapon to keep the opponents away from the body, the best way being to use it bent at the elbow in the form of a shield with which you can hit an opponent before he hits you. It can also be used as a straight arm to push players away, but it is much easier for tacklers to grab onto when used this way. Remember that tacklers are trying basically to use the same hitting principles as used in blocking, so a ball carrier must either avoid the hit or hit himself first before the opponent is on balance ready to deliver his own blow.

Moves or cuts to avoid tacklers should be made with the weight of the body over the leg away from the way you want to run. Then if a hit is made while cutting, the other leg will take the weight in its turn and balance may still be maintained. In this way the hit may actually help you change direction as you wanted.

The free hand can also be useful in avoiding going to the ground by pushing on the ground when balance is lost just before the back falls. This is a difficult technique, but should be practiced in a drill in which the back runs forward slowly carrying a ball and every 5 yards puts his free hand to the ground and pushes himself back up to running position, continuing to do this for about 30 yards. The drill should be repeated often. This drill can also be combined with a drill to help backs cut properly over the correct leg. In this combined drill the back carrying a ball makes a 45-degree change of direction every 5 yards, changing hands with the ball while cutting and dropping the free hand to the ground and pushing back into balance. This drill should be done slowly at first, but as the players get used to the feeling of losing their balance and regaining it, they get the feeling for making the cuts naturally over the correct leg and in balance. The speed of the cuts can be increased along with the competence of the player.

Another good drill that helps a back learn to hold onto the ball and maintain balance while being hit is the following:

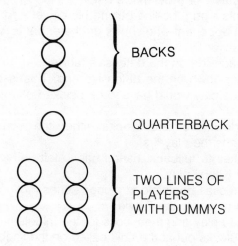

The quarterback hands off the ball to a back who immediately has to run the guantlet of two lines of players each with a small dummy. The players in the two lines either hit the ball carrier with the dummy or put the dummy on their forearms and try to knock the runner off balance.

TYPICAL RUNNING PLAY

We can now use our knowledge of numbering and running techniques to go through a typical running play player by player. With this play the blocking assignments of the lineman are outlined, bearing in mind that there are several ways to block along the line. Let's look at our old play, "Plunge 27."

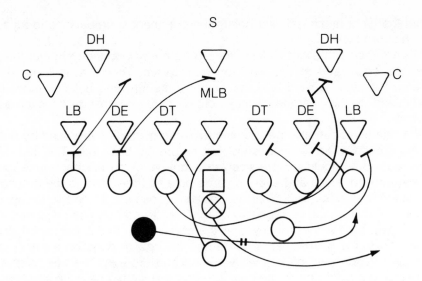

Duties of Each Player

Left End: The end is in tight on this play, but he might just as easily have split 5 or 7 yards. The left end tries to get across the field between the safety and the ball carrier to block.

Left Tackle: Blocks the defensive and momentarily and then goes down field to block either the safety or a defensive back.

Left Guard: Sprints along the line behind his player and turns up through the 7 hole, hits the first opponent who shows up there, but is watching specifically for the middle linebacker.

Center: Blocks backside on the defensive tackle.

Right End: Blocks down on the defensive end. This is a tough block for most tight ends, and the play would have to be blocked differently if the end couldn't execute it.

Flanker: Runs downfield and blocks either the corner or defensive half, whichever threatens the play first.

Quarterback: Fakes to fullback, hands ball to left half and continues to fake a "19 Quarterback Keep" play.

Left Halfback: Crosses backfield in plunge series motion, is handed the ball by quarterback and runs into the 7 hole.

Fullback: Fakes 30 play and then looks for the middle linebacker to block.

Right Halfback: Blocks out at the hole called on the linebacker.

PASS RECEIVING

All backs must learn to catch the ball and become good pass receivers. In fact, on some teams backs are the leading receivers, for it is always shorter to throw to the backs than it is to throw to the wide receivers.

Pass receiving

STANCE

The stance for a back on a pass play should be the same as for a running play. However, if the play calls for the back either in the slot or the wing position to split out more than 4 yards from the nearest down lineman, he can use the two-point stance. A wide receiver may use either the two- or three-point stance.

Two-point stance

RELEASING TECHNIQUES   For Slot Backs, Wing Backs and Tight Ends

Always anticipate the snap count. You know when the ball is coming out, so you have an advantage on the defense. The defense will likely try to hold you up from establishing your pattern, so you must practice the following techniques to get free. Remember, unless you establish your pattern, the play will not come off.

1. Vary your split. This will allow you to release on the inside at times rather than the usual release outside the linebacker.

2. Release hard and expect to get hit, even though you may not have been on similar plays previously.

3. Fake block and then release.

4. Fake block, pivot and release.

5. Fake one way and go the other.

6. Submarine. Drop to all fours, get up, and go. This technique is useful on a delay-type pattern, as the defense might lose sight of you when you're down.

RUNNING INDIVIDUAL PASS PATTERNS

A pass receiver must be a good actor. You must not let on to the defense that a pass play has been called until the quarterback drops back to pass. When leaving the huddle you should look over the defensive alignment on every play for clues to the type of defense being set up against you (zone or man-on-man are important distinctions on a pass play).

Pass patterns are run in three stages:

1. Start fast to make the defender retreat.

2. Ease up to about three-quarters speed to execute your move. Make quick moves. Fake about two yards from the defensive man and break sharply.
    — Make the defender run in the opposite direction from your final break.
    — In faking use: speed

    > eyes
    > head and shoulders
    > hips
    > feet (jab step in direction opposite to final break; fake one way and roll off rear leg toward defender).

    — Always run the pass pattern called by the quarterback.
    — Use speed and deception to get into the open.
    — Run your pattern deep enough to get first-down yardage.
    — Observe the defensive man playing against you to find out:
        — How deep is the defender covering you?
        — Is he lined up with your inside or outside shoulder?
        — How fast is he?
        — Does he go for a first fake?
        — Does he watch the passes or keep his eyes on you?
        — Can you beat him deep outside or deep inside?
        — Does he leave you quickly once he thinks that a running play has been called?
        — How is his cover on a man-on-man and zone?
        — What is his first reaction on a pass?
        — Learn something about the defender on each fake.

3. A burst of speed is important. Get a one-step advantage on the defender, even when acting as a decoy. Don't loaf. Make sure you know and execute all stages for the pass patterns. Otherwise, the defender will know when you are faking.

Pattern Stages

1. Start

2. Fake/Execution

3. Speed

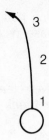

RECEIVING

— "No pass play is successful until the ball is caught."
— Relax the whole body momentarily before catching the ball.
— Concentrate — think *only* of catching the ball.
— Keep both eyes on the ball, *look the ball into your hands.* "See it."
— Never take your eyes off a thrown ball.
— Do not extend arms to catch the ball until the ball arrives.
— Catch the ball the easiest, most natural way — relax your hands.
— Hands should "give" with the ball.
— Catch with your hands: Thumbs out when running away from ball, thumbs in when facing passer.
— On hooks, step towards the passer.
— On long passes, don't let one arm blind you.
— Always take ball at its highest point.
— Expect a bad pass (always be prepared to react to a poorly thrown pass).
— If you can't catch the ball, don't allow the opponent to catch it.
— Fight for possession of the ball.
— Get into the air; use your body.

The ball will be thrown quicker and area will be clear if defense is playing for the run.

RUNNING WITH BALL

— Carry the ball properly.
— Never fumble.
— Move straight to the opponent's goal.
— Use blockers.
— Don't try to dodge an opponent until you are near him.
— Keep your legs churning and driving.
— Get the first down; get to the opponent's goal.

PASS ROUTES

1. Hook

Receiver clears to the outside as if to be running a go. He reaches the required depth for a normal hook, 9 to 11 yards. He then plants his outside foot firmly and steps back toward the quarterback and approximately 1 yard inside. The ball should be on its way as the receiver is turning. If the ball is not on its way, the receiver should slide right or left depending on the play of linebackers. It is essential that the receiver does not back up on a hook pattern. He must be sure he hooks for first down yardage.

2. Flag

Clearing pattern. Receiver comes off the line, up the field 15 yards. One step fake inside, runs to the flag.

3. Post

Receiver clears to the outside, turns up the field 8 yards. One step fake inside, break to the goal post. Look over your inside shoulder.

4. Corner

Receiver clears to the outside, turns up the field 8 yards. One step fake outside, two, three, or four step fake inside, break to the corner of the field.

5. Slant In

Receiver clears up the field 4 yards, breaks in under the clearing man and cuts off the linebacker at a 45-degree angle up the field. Outside foot — inside foot — outside foot — cut.

6. Look In

Receiver comes off the line into an open spot looking "immediately" over his inside shoulder at the quarterback.

7. Hitch

Receiver clears the line. Turns in to the quarterback, steps back, making the target.

8. Shallow

The receiver clears quickly to his outside at a 45-degree angle never getting deeper than 4 yards, looking over outside shoulder toward the Q.B.

9. Shallow and Up

Receiver clears to his outside at a 45-degree angle never getting deeper than 4 yards, then he clears out about 8 yards. He looks over his outside shoulder at the quarterback as if to catch the ball and then looks over his inside shoulder, turns up the field getting as deep as he possibly can.

10. Stop

Receiver clears to the outside, trying to get the defender to widen with him. At about 12 to 15 yards, he then plants his outside foot and turns immediately to the inside looking for the ball. He continues to the inside to create a passing lane. When the passing lane is open, the he stops and moves toward the quarterback. The passing lane can open up as soon as he curls to the inside. The receiver must be prepared to receive the ball immediately on his curl. This is true versus tight man-to-man defense.

11. Break-Out

Receiver clears to the outside and goes up the field 10 yards. Fake inside and break out to the sideline at an angle slightly less than 90-degrees and continue going to the sideline at full speed.

12. Break-In

This pattern is almost the opposite to a break-out. Receiver clears the line at full speed, gains control, and breaks at 90-degrees or just a little more depending on how the linebackers are playing.

13. Come Back

Receiver clears to the outside, turns up the field 10 to 12 yards. Three or four steps fake outside, comes back at a sharp angle to the ball. It is the responsibility of the receiver to make sure he gets the first down yardage on the come back.

14. Bootleg

Run relaxed "break-out flag" type action. Quarterback may decide to run. Be ready to block on red call.

15. Go

Clearing pattern. Receiver comes off the line straight up the field 15 yards, one step fake outside, continues running up the field looking over inside shoulder.

Motion or Peel

One pass pattern used exclusively by backs is the motion or peel pattern. This pattern is often called the flare or swing pass, but since these names can be used to describe other patterns, we will avoid using them for the sake of clarity.

Halfback or fullback "swings" to zone looking immediately over his inside shoulder at the quarterback. The back continues to look and it is the back's responsibility to keep looking at the quarterback. On the swing route never get more than 5 to 6 yards deep from the line of scrimmage. The receiver must make a good target by being able to turn his shoulders and chest partially toward the quarterback.

Any man in the backfield can go in motion and run almost any of the individual patterns. The names of these patterns vary at times from team to team, so it is wise to learn the terminology for the offensive plan you maybe involved in rather than just learning the names in this book.

INDIVIDUAL PASS PATTERNS

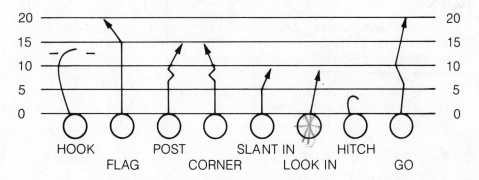

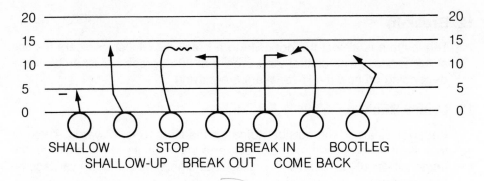

SHALLOW   STOP   BREAK IN   BOOTLEG
    SHALLOW-UP   BREAK OUT   COME BACK

Patterns With Two Receivers

The individual patterns or routes already described can be combined with those of other receivers to make a pass pattern. These patterns may be called by any convenient name and must be memorized by the name given to the offensive set-up your team uses. Following are diagrams of patterns for two receivers on one side of the field. The receiver or receivers on the other side run complementary patterns, patterns that will not interfere with the receivers in areas already covered.

DOUBLE PATTERNS FOR WINGBACK OR TIGHT END AND FLANKER BACK
(ALSO SPLIT END AND SLOT BACK)

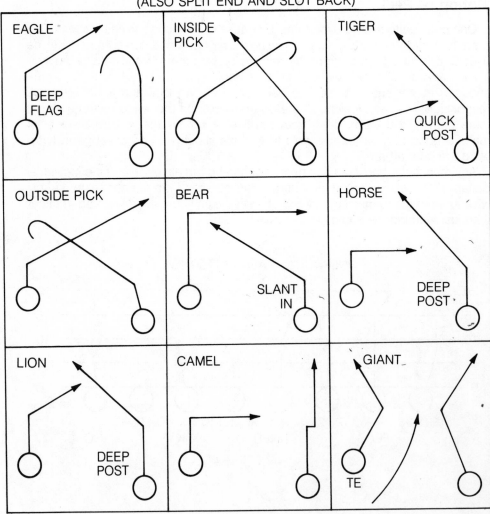

Triple Patterns

A triple pattern is a pass pattern in which three receivers on the same side of the field are involved. These three receivers may be the flanker, wingback, and tight end or the slotbacks, split end, and a back coming out of the backfield. Also, a back may come out of the backfield to combine with the tight end and flanker to run a triple pattern. Some samples of this type of pattern follow:

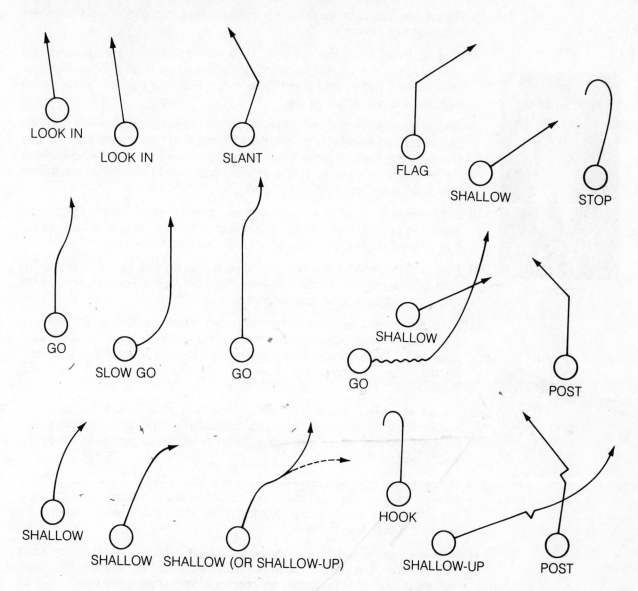

BASIC PRINCIPLES FOR PASS RECEIVERS

1. Keep your eyes on the ball. Your first responsibility is to *catch the ball. After* you make the catch, think about additional yardage and scoring.

2. When you are on offense and the ball is thrown, it is *not* a "free" ball. IT is *Yours – Go Get It*! Never allow an interception. Anything goes.

3. Whenever possible, catch the ball in your hands, not against your chest.

Equipment

4. In practice, after you catch the ball, tuck it away securely and SPRINT at least 10 yards. Put in a fake, spin, etc.; simulate what you would do in a game.

5. When you warm up, don't just jog around. Run in spurts, change of pace, weaves, cuts, stutter steps, etc. Start from your stance. Use head fakes to release from imaginary linebackers.

6. Always run your patterns at full, controlled speed. You cannot get the correct timing at half speed.

7. Pass receivers are made, not born. They are made by practice day after day until all of the moves and receiving become second nature. Whenever possible, have a ball in your hands. Play catch with your partner. Never let the ball become a stranger to you.

8. Always be alert for the ball, even though you are not the primary receiver. You never know when the quarterback will throw to you! Do not loaf because you think the pass is going to someone else. Carry out your assignment at full speed on every play. This is an easy way to tell the difference between the "good ones" and the "great ones."

9. Concentrate at all times on what you are going to do — why and how you are going to do it. Keep in mind the object of the pass and what your part of it is. Know the complete picture, not just your part of the play.

10. Talk to the quarterback when you have a chance (not in the huddle). Tell your coaches what you can do — your best bet for third-down passes, third and 7 to 10 yards, your best long pattern.

11. Learn the tendencies of the defensive backs; if they gamble, guess with you, play tight or loose, inside or out, their speed. *Have a "book" on all of your opponents.* Be an artist in your profession. Know the defensive team tendencies; how they cover first down, second and third, short and long yardage, etc.

12. Always know field position (sideline), time remaining, down and distance, sun position, wind conditions, lights, condition of field (high or low) spots, pitcher's mound, infield dirt, ball position in regard to goal posts (they are your friends).

13. The sidelines and end-zone lines are enemies. Always know your relative position to them. Respect them, but do not let them bother you in catching the ball — the catch comes the first. The officials will never call you "in bounds" if you drop the ball.

14. Always expect to get hit after, or as, you catch the ball — then the jolt won't surprise you. You have to "want it." You catch the ball and pay the price. You must have utter disregard for contact while catching the ball.

15. Always be alert for clotheslines and "cut" blocks.

16. After a diving catch, remember "up and go." The opponent has to knock you down.

17. When you are breaking past a defensive man and have him beat, be alert for holding or tackling. They are taught to take the penalty rather than the touchdown. *You must clear them.* You can get away with a push or straight arm in this situation.

18. Get in the habit of going all out after the ball every time, regardless of how it is thrown. Soon the great catches will become routine.

19. Fake the man, not the area.

20. Receivers are football players, not just pass catchers. BLOCK!!!

THE KICKING GAME

Zenon Andrusyshyn, Toronto Argonauts

ZENON ANDRUSYSHYN

Zenon was born in Gunzburg, Germany. He attended college at UCLA, and while there received the NCAA punting award in 1967, was selected *Sporting News* All-American in 1967 and 1969, and Pacific 8 All-Conference and all-time kicker for UCLA for the past 50 years. He was a 9th round draft choice of the Dallas Cowboys in 1970, and joined the Argos in 1971.

In 1972 Zenon punted 258 times for 11,405 yards and a 44.2 yard average. In 1973 he punted 121 times for a 45.6 yard average. He was also the Argos leading scorer with 100 points on 25 of 26 converts, 19 of 37 field goals and 18 singles.

"Let's face it, this isn't a very good life if your team keeps kicking from the end zone, where you have to run so far from the bench."

Sam Baker, St. Louis Cardinals

"I don't want anyone talking to me during the game unless it's something about the field or wind that I may have missed. I stand in my own area at the end of the bench. People don't get too close to me. I have to be left alone so that when my moment comes I have the best frame of mind when I step on the field."

Zenon Andrusyshyn, Toronto Argonauts

THE KICKING GAME

Kicking is one of the most important parts of a football game, yet it is also the part that receives the least attention from the media. Without sound kicking the chances of winning a championship are slight.

Your kicking game is a part of your offensive arsenal as well as part of your defensive strength. From the offensive point of view, the field goal is a potent weapon. Those teams without a competent field goal team are indeed handicapped. From the defensive side, the punting game in Canadian football plays an important role. When playing deep in your own end, a good punt on a third-down situation will keep the ball away from your goal line. On the other hand, the ability of your special team — to block the field goal, to defend against the punt, and to rush the kicker — must be sconsidered vital to the defense of any team.

All aspects of the kicking game are parts of the individual commitment to excellence that a player must make. It takes a total team effort for the kicker to get off a good kick, as it does to block a kick. Team effort is the basis of all aspects of football.

KICKING FUNDAMENTALS

A kicker must have the same physical and mental characteristics as other football players. He should be big enough to withstand the contact of the game, have strong legs, possess speed and toughness as a coverage man and agility and quickness as a safety man. He must also be a hard worker, willing to practice his art. And, like everyone else on the team, he must be coachable. The fact that he is a kicker on a professional team doesn't mean that he has nothing more to learn. There are exceptions to all of these rules, of course, and Garo Yepremian at 5′6″ and 160 pounds, and Tom Dempsey at 6′4″ and 275 pounds, are good examples of the extreme physical characteristics of kickers. In essence, then, a small man with ability is able to become an excellent professional kicker.

There are three different kicking situations in the game: the punt, the point after touchdown and field goal, and the kickoff. I will deal with the basics of each individually and point out how to get off your best kick in each situation.

PUNTING

At no time should a punter ever be concerned with the rush from the defense. This is a primary rule. There is enough to concentrate on without being worried about the rush. Obviously there are times when a blocker will get through, and the kick will be blocked, but the odds against this are very high.

Receiving the punt

Once the ball is received from the center it should be brought into position quickly in front and across the body at hip level. The heel of the ball should be covered with the palm of the right hand with the thumb at midseam. The nose of the ball should be cradled in the left hand. Receiving the snap must be done quickly, as you only have about two seconds to get the ball away.

Your first step is with the kicking foot, which should be pointed forward in a straight line with the goal line (1). Your plant foot takes the next step (2). This is your control foot, and should also be in a straight line forward. You will contact the ball on the third step (See diagram below).

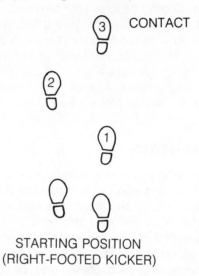

STARTING POSITION
(RIGHT-FOOTED KICKER)

You are now in a position to kick. The next phase is the most important part of kicking — the drop. A proper drop will result in a good kick; a poor drop will spin the ball off the side of your foot. Your right hand should control the ball and act as a guide for the release. The left hand acts only to support the ball.

Holding the ball

The Drop

— Place index fingers down the side of the ball. The front hand should be taken away first.
— Ball should drop in a smooth arch to the kicking foot.
— Ball should be parallel to ground.

| *First step* | *Second step* | *Third step* |

— For high kicks, ball and foot contact should occur no lower than 6″ below the waist.
— For lower, longer kicks, contact the ball at a lower point.
— Meet the ball with the outside of the foot.

| *Foot meeting ball* | *Momentum* |

— The kicking leg should be cocked with the toe parallel to the ground. Get your power from the knee and arch the instep.
— The leg whip should carry the kicking foot as far as possible after contact.
— Your momentum should force the entire body to raise up and out toward the direction of the punt.

If the punt is properly executed, a good long spiraling kick can be heard as well as seen. It will sound more like a thud than a big boom. I stress that the follow-through is a must. It is only with a proper follow-through that the punter can get maximum distance out of his kicks, particularly if the height of the kick is more important on a particular play than the distance.

Punting

Spread Punt-Coaching Points

1. Kicker will call "Punt — on the ball!"

2. Everyone will assume a two-point stance.

3. Splits:
   a. Guards — about 2 yards (Space of a man)
   b. Tackles — about 2 yards
   c. Ends — about 2 yards
   d. Slotbacks — 1 yard deep
   e. Fullback — 6 yards deep, directly behind the right slotback (Unless left foot kicker)
   f. Kicker — 14 yards deep.

4. When everyone is set, the fullback will check to see if kicker is ready. He will then call "Ready!" No one can move after call of "Ready!"

5. Center will snap any time after call of "Ready!" Vary rhythm so defense cannot anticipate and get a jump on a punt block attempt.

6. Timing:
   a. Snap should reach punter in 9.7 seconds.
   b. Punter takes maximum of 1.3 seconds to kick after receiving snap.
   c. Ball should remain in the air at least 4.0 seconds and be 45 yards or more from the line of scrimmage to be considered a good kick.

Punt Coverage Coaching Points

1. Maintain 5-yard lanes between man on either side.

2. Break down 5 yards in front of punt returner, until he touches ball.

3. You must cover a blocked punt that goes beyond line of scrimmage.

4. Blocked punt that stays on our side of the line of scrimmage — try to recover ball and run for the first down.

Punt Block Coaching Points

SPREAD PUNT BLOCKING

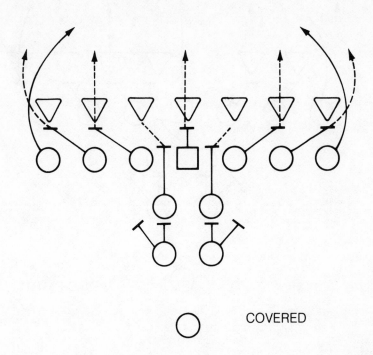

COVERED

SPREAD PUNT BLOCKING

GAPPED

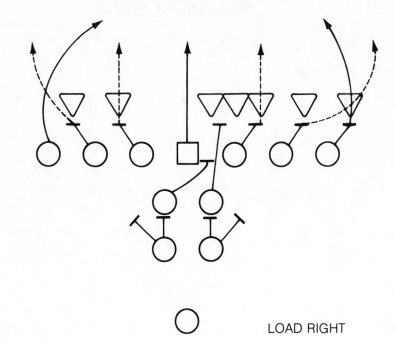

LOAD RIGHT

"HELP CALL"

LOAD RIGHT

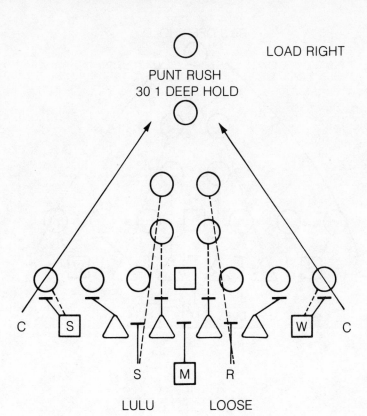

PUNT RUSH
30 1 DEEP HOLD

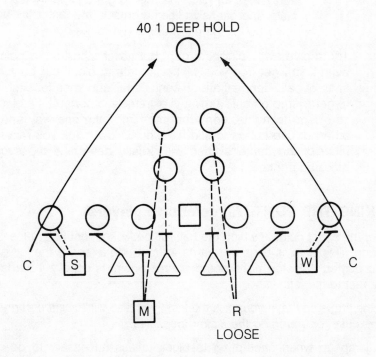

40 1 DEEP HOLD

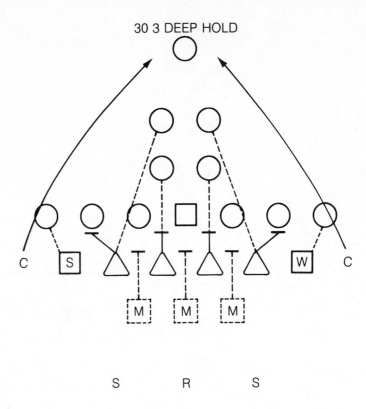

30 3 DEEP HOLD

S   R   S

Up Front Lineman — Start on snap of ball as fast as possible. Watch center's tail and knees for hitch in order to get a jump on the ball. The faster the offensive lineman block, the faster the holes will open up for the pluggers to get to the punter.

Pluggers — Try to give away plugging gap, but never start from a point where even if you get free you will be too late to block the punt. Start on snap of ball. Concentrate on center's tail and knee for hitch in order to get a jump on ball. Timing is extremely important. If a blocker has you dead to rights, don't run into him. Fake one way and go the other: or use hands to slip his block. How quick you move on the hitch of the center's knee will greatly determine the success in blocking punts.

BLOCKING THE PUNT (All defensive players)

1. Aim for the exact point at which the ball will be kicked, not where the punter is standing. This point is usually *3 yards* in front and *2 feet* to the left of a right footed punter. A 3-step right-footed punter's point is usually 4 yards in front and 2 feet to the left.

2. Take the angle so that if you miss the kick, you also will *miss the punter. There is no excuse for 'roughing the kicker' penalties.*

3. Don't jump up when attempting to block unless necessary to go over the deep blocker. Either *run through* kicking point or *dive out* in order to reach the kicking point with your hands as soon as possible.

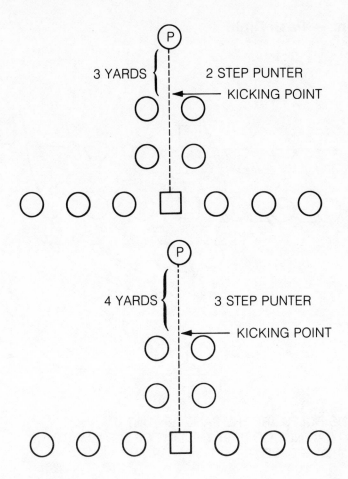

4. Keep your eyes open! Try to look kicked ball into outstretched hands. Almost all 'roughing the kicker' penalties and missed blocked punts that could have been blocked are the result of closing the eyes.

5. After blocking the punt, try to pick it up and advance it toward the goal line. Never fall on the ball unless it is completely surrounded by players.

6. The remaining players block the kicker so that he cannot tackle the player who picks up the ball to advance it for a touchdown.

Added Dimension of the Punts

Many times during the course of a season the punter can pull his team out of a hole by faking a punt and either passing or running. This fake punt play is usually called from the sidelines, and places a great deal of responsibility on the rest of the team. If the play is unsuccessful, your team will be left in a very bad field position.

In a fake punt situation the punter goes through his normal routine, but at the last moment throws either to a back who is swinging out or to an end who is downfield far enough to get a first down. If the punter decides to run he must get the first down himself. Since the blockers will still be coming in as if there was a punt, the punter must realize that he has to avoid these defenders first before picking up yards. Therefore, it is better to pass from a fake punt situation, but the punter must exercise good judgment to know when he can pull and run with the ball.

Fake Punt — Pass Right

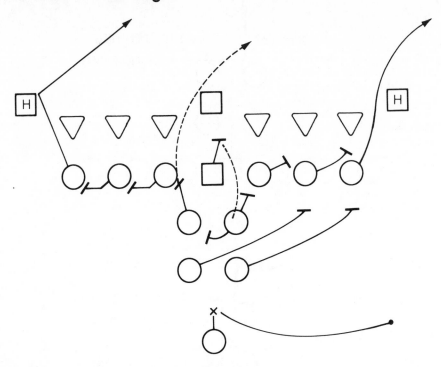

1. BLOCKING RULES ARE THE SAME AS PUNT
2. LINEMEN CAN NOT GO PAST THE LINE OF SCRIMMAGE (UNLESS BALL IS EVENTUALLY KICKED.)

Weather Problems

1. *Rain and mud.* Poor weather conditions always cause problems for kickers, and anyone playing in Canada or the northern United States can expect to encounter bad weather. In rain or muddy conditions, the ball will be slippery, and an extra effort must be made to field the snap and place it on the foot. It is perfectly legal to have a towel to wipe your shoes and hands. Use longer cleats under these conditions, but watch yourself when kicking, for even the best cleats won't prevent you from slipping at times and ruining the kick.

    Rain can be an asset, however, If you are aiming for the corner away from the punt return men, the ball will bounce especially well on wet astro turf. You might be able to pick up a little distance.

Point of contact into wind

Normal position

Normal position, rear view

Kicking with the wind

2. *Wind*. Most punters don't practice kicking into the wind, and will find themselves in a jam if there is a strong wind at game time. When kicking into the wind, the ball must be dropped absolutely parallel to the ground. It should be contacted at a lower spot than on a normal punt. This keeps the ball down, as high punts into the wind tend to stall. Try to spiral the ball, because a spiral usually travels a lot further than an end-over-end kick. Because of the extra time it takes to get a punt off into the wind, the punt rush tends to get in a step closer. Release the ball as quickly as possible.

3. *Snow and Sleet*. Because of the cold, the ball tends not to be as elastic as usual. You will have to kick harder to get the same distance out of your punt. But remember that the ground is usually slippery, so be careful not to over-stride and slip.

   Try not to let your muscles tighten up in the cold. Keep yourself warm by wearing gloves on the sidelines. Long underwear will also help.

FIELD GOAL AND POINT AFTER TOUCHDOWN

BASIC ALIGNMENT

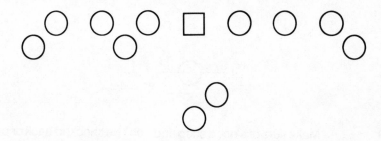

While the punter's main objective is distance and height, that of the field goal kicker and point after touchdown kicker is accuracy. Of course, a field goal may have to be attempted from quite a distance as well, especially late in the game with your team behind, so don't forget about distance.

There are two main types of kickers, those who use the orthodox style of kick and those who use the soccer style. These styles may be broken down into:
  (i) Power kicker (kicks with power and no form)
  (ii) Puncher (leg kicker, no follow through)
  (iii) Form kicker (uses body, has greater control and power)

Paying attention to the wind and the position of the ball on the field, the kicker has to aim the ball at a point where the ball will pass mid-way between the uprights. An imaginary line can be drawn from the ball right through the goal posts.

FIELD GOAL TEAM

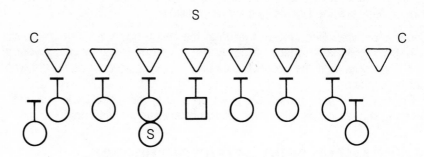

CENTER	Make sure of a good snap and don't be knocked back or pulled.
GUARD TACKLE ENDS	Three-point stance, no splits, and at snap of the ball, chop step in place with inside footband; make yourself big.
WING BACKS	Two-point stance and at snap of the ball, make yourself big and tensify.
HOLDER	Get ready call from kicker and give ready call to team. Ball is snapped on center's snap.
SLOT BACK	Line up in two-point stance behind offensive left guard; block first dangerous man to overload side.

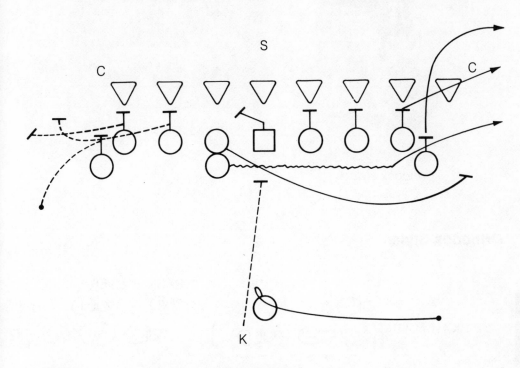

KICKER	Fake kick, protect middle.
RIGHT END	Hold position, release to shallow flat.
LEFT END	Protect for 3 count, release as screen.
LEFT TACKLE	Protect for 3 count, release as screen.
RIGHT WING	Run fan or corner, get open
LEFT WING	Protect and delay 3 counts, release as screen. Catch ball about 5 yards outside, 4 yards deep.
HOLDER	Throw right if open. Pull up and execute screen option if right pattern covered.
LINEMAN	Use P.P. 2-3 trap protection. Off guard pull for most dangerous man to outside.

Orthodox style

Soccer style

Orthodox Style

Orthodox approach

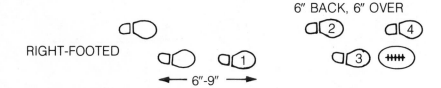

RIGHT-FOOTED

6″ BACK, 6″ OVER

← 6″-9″ →

1. First step 6 to 9 inches (to align with goal posts) with kicking foot.

2. Second step varies with kicker but should allow the plant foot to land 6 inches back and 6 inches wide of the ball.

3. The toe should be cocked perpendicular to the ground (ankle locked).

4. The body should be over the ball perpendicular to the ground. You should not lean back or lie too far over the ball.

Soccer Style

This style of kicking varies, but as a rule of thumb take two steps back from the ball and one step to the left if right-footed, vice-versa if left-footed.

Approach — Soccer Style

1. Step 2 feet to 3 feet toward ball with kicking foot.
2. Second step should align the left foot about 6 feet away from ball but parallel to it. The toe of the left foot should be pointing at the goal posts.
3. Body position — at an angle and slightly back to achieve a whip action in the leg.

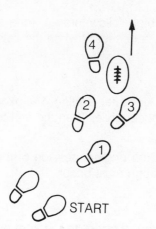

Soccer-style approach

Contact

Whether using either the orthodox or the soccer style approach, the ball should be hit approximately 1 inch below center. The angle of the ball in relation to the kicker's foot varies from kicker to kicker. This will alter the contact point on the ball, but not drastically enough to cause any problems.

Soccer-style contact

Orthodox-style contact

Follow-Through

Follow-through, soccer style

Follow-through, orthodox style

This is a very important phase in kicking. A high follow-through (one that is natural) gets the ball into the air high and fast, a necessity when the field goal rush is on.

1. Keep the head down

2. Feet should be pointed in the direction of the kick after landing. The exception to this rule occurs when the ball is kicked soccer style. Then the feet tend to drift in a different direction.

3. The follow-through will carry the kicker past the original position of the ball. This is your clue to a good kick. A follow-through must occur.

HOLDING FOR THE KICKER

The holder lines up with his left knee on the ground opposite the spot whence the kicker is going to boot the ball, and puts the fingertips of his left hand on the spot where the ball will be placed. He then extends his right hand 2 feet off the ground towards the center in order to present a target. The holder should never take the marking hand off the ground until the ball is snapped. This gives the kicker a target as well.

Holding approach

Holding contact

The snap should come low enough to the ground that when the holder gets it, the ball will be about knee high. When the holder catches the ball, he places it on the ground, his left hand holding the point and his right hand spiraling the ball to make the laces forward. Under no circumstances should the laces face the kicker. There should be enough pressure on top of the ball to hold it steady until kicked.

There is approximately 1.3 seconds between the time the ball is caught and the time that it is kicked to get the kick off comfortably and prevent a block.

KICKING OFF

The ball is kicked from a tee (1-inch tee in Canadian football, 2-inch in American) to begin the game and the third quarter, and after a touchdown. As with the punt and the field goal, it is important to get distance in your kick to drive the opposition as far away from your goal line as possible.

There is a basic sequence which the kicker should follow on the kick-off. This sequence varies slightly from those we have discussed previously.

1. The ball should lean 1 to 2 inches on the tee towards the kicker.

2. Use at least 7 steps.

3. Begin to step slowly and deliberately with your kicking foot in order not to miss your step prior to contact.

4. Eye-to-ball concentration should be focused 5¼ inches from the top of the ball.

5. Plant fast 9 inches back and 6 inches to the side of the ball.

6. Kicking foot should be locked on contact with the ball.

7. Follow through. The contact foot should swing through the ball with the ankle locked until at least waist high. The plant foot should be forced off the ground by your momentum to land 6 inches in front of the tee.

The Kick Off

94

KICK OFF SEQUENCE

KICK OFF RETURN TEAM

LEFT   RIGHT

L5 L4 L3 L2 L1   K   R1 R2 R3 R4 R5

45 ——————————————————————— 45

55 ——————————————————————— 55
        LT   LG   C   RG   RT
50 ——————————————————————— 50

45 ——————————————————————— 45
   LE   LB   RB   RE
40 ——————————————————————— 40

35 ——————————————————————— 35

30 ——————————————————————— 30

25 ——————————————————————— 25
              MB
20 ——————————————————————— 20

15 ——————————————————————— 15

10 ——————————————————————— 10
          LS   RS
5 ——————————————————————— 5

PROCEDURE

1. Huddle on 40-yard line and get return call.

2. Center — Captain count players.

3. Do not be offside (10 yards from kick).

4. Be alert for onside kick. Be sure to recover any kick that goes 10 yards or more anywhere on playing field (including end zone) unless ball is definitely going out of bounds.

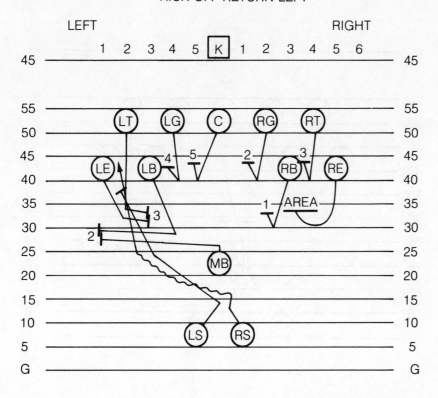

PROCEDURE

CENTER   Blocks L5

RIGHT GUARD   Blocks R2

LEFT GUARD   Blocks L4

RIGHT TACKLE   Blocks

LEFT TACKLE   Blocks L3

RIGHT END   Blocks area

LEFT END   Blocks L3

LEFT BACKER   Blocks L2

RIGHT BACKER   Blocks R1

MIDDLE BACKER Blocks L2

BACK NOT CARRYING BALL — personal interference

BALL CARRIER   Start upfield like middle return, then follow your personal inter-
                ferer.

NOTE: If ball is kicked outside of opposite hash mark, return to that side.

KICK OFF RETURN MIDDLE

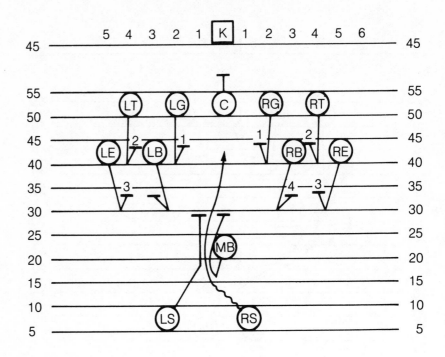

PROCEDURE

GENERAL INFORMATION

1. Count inside out 1-6 from kicker or middle man.

2. This is a middle return. Ball carrier finds daylight.

3. The first wave (G and T) turns at 40-yard line and blocks your assigned man.

4. The second waves (E and B) turn at 30-yard line and block your assigned man.

5. The lead blockers (B and S) lead interference for ball carrier.

6. Ball carrier must get upfield fast so he won't be picked off from side or behind.

RULES

CENTER	Fire out and knock kicker down.
GUARDS	Block 1 man to your side of kicker.
TACKLES	Block 2 man to your side of kicker.
ENDS	Block 3 man to your side of kicker.
LB & RB	Block 4 man to your side of kicker.

MB & BACK NOT CARRYING BALL — personal interference for ball carrier.

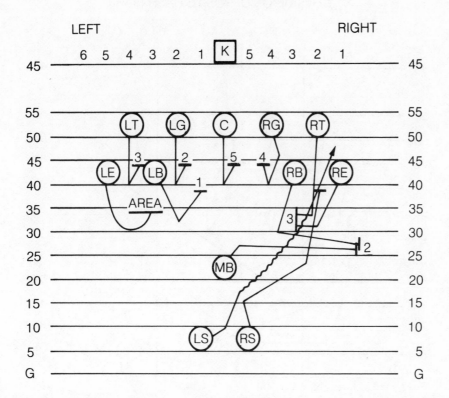

PROCEDURE

CENTER	Blocks R5
RIGHT GUARD	Blocks R4
LEFT GUARD	Blocks L2
RIGHT TACKLE	Blocks R3
LEFT TACKLE	Blocks L3
RIGHT END	Blocks R3
LEFT END	Blocks area
LEFT BACKER	Blocks L1
RIGHT BACKER	Blocks R2
MIDDLE BACKER	Blocks R2

BACK NOT CARRYING BALL — Personal interferer

BALL CARRIER   Start upfield like middle return, then follow your personal interferer.

NOTE: If ball is kicked outside of opposite hash mark, return to that side.

KICK OFF RETURN RIGHT WITH BALL KICKED OUTSIDE OF OPPOSITE HASH MARK

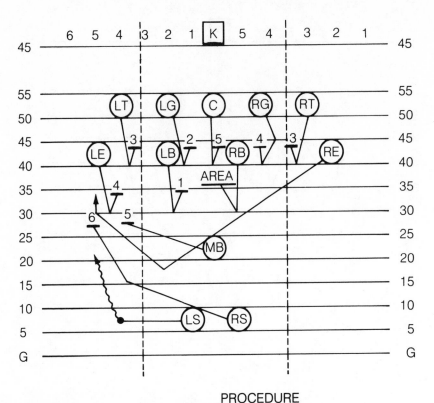

PROCEDURE

CENTER	Blocks R5
RIGHT GUARD	Blocks R4
LEFT GUARD	Blocks L2
RIGHT TACKLE	Blocks R3
LEFT TACKLE	Blocks L3
RIGHT END	Blocks area
LEFT END	Blocks L4
LEFT BACKER	
RIGHT BACKER	
MIDDLE BACKER	
BACK NOT CARRYING BALL — Blocks L6 or outside man	
BALL CARRIER	Locate ball, get upfield fast, and run to daylight.

Onside Kicks

The onside kick is used when your team is forced to retain the ball, and must be backed short in an attempt to recover it. This kick must be perfectly executed in order to be successful. The ball must go 10 yards before your team can recover, and since the defenders are waiting for a kick they are in a good position to recover it. If the onside kick is unsuccessful, your team will lose valuable field position.

It must appear to the defending team that you are going to kick long. Otherwise, they will be ready for your onside kick.

1. Instep kick: Slice the ball with the instep of the foot. With the same amount of momentum as for a normal kick-off, you will be using less force. The ball should only travel about 10 yards.

Ground kick

ONSIDE KICK PREVENT

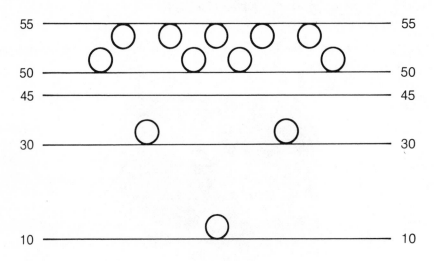

PROCEDURE

1. Watch ball.

2. If ball does not come to you, block, push, pull.

3. Just recover — no runback.

4. Outside man — cover over man who recovers ball.

5. Win the game defense. Deep backs — no runback. Go down — we want the ball — not a return. Take touchback.

CHECKLISTS FOR KICKING FAULTS

Punting

1. High punt: ball contacted above waist.

2. Low Punt: ball contacted low below knee.

3. End over end: nose or heel of ball too low. Ball should be paralell to ground.

4. Ball goes left: ball contacted too close and to the left of body.

5. Ball goes right: ball kicked to the extreme right of body.

Field Goal, Point after Touchdown

1. High kick: Ball will spin excessively if contacted too low. Body too far over ball.

2. Low kick: Contact point too high. Holder does not put enough angle on ball. Body leaning back.

3. Ball does not spin end over end: ball contacted dead center.

4. Ball goes left: ball contacted on right side.

5. Ball goes right: ball contacted on left side.

KICKING SCHEDULE

Pre-Season

From my own experience, I find that beginning a pre-season workout schedule has a lot to do with the weather. My initial training is usually done with weights or in some form of indoor sport such as squash or handball. Around May, when your wind and stamina have been built up a bit, begin a serious outdoor running program, and begin your kicking schedule. Work strictly on form, and don't attempt any strenuous kicking for about a month. A good pre-season workout schedule could include weight training, calisthenics, stretching, jogging for a mile, 6 to 10 sprints of 50 yards each, and 30 to 60 minutes of form kicking.

Season

During the season your kicking should be near perfect. Don't ignore fundamentals, however. You should develop yourself to become like a finely tuned machine, ready for any game situation. During practices, kick field goals with the center at the 37, 47, and 57 yard lines. Kicking from these distances forces you to depend on your style as well as power. It is from these distances that your style usually falls apart. Practice kicking with a full rush in order to simulate game conditions. And don't forget exercises to keep in shape and to develop your kicking. Any of the exercises described later in this chapter, along with the drills, are important.

DAY OF THE GAME

1. Have a good meal about 4 to 5 hours before the game. You don't have to eat a steak; most players have individual tastes and eat as much or as little as suits them.

2. Reach the stadium early enough to prepare yourself mentally for the game. Again, this varies from player to player. Some go early, others late.

3. Before the game try to visualize your entire kicking game. This is another aspect of mental preparation. Think positively.

4. Spend between half an hour to an hour warming up in the dressing room. As a kicker, stretching exercises are more important to you than to the other players, so concentrate on them. There are a number of good stretching exercises in the calisthenics section of this chapter.

During the Game

1. Since you as a kicker will only be needed at certain times, it is nice to be warmed up during the entire game. Maintain a high level of concentration throughout the game. You might be called into the game late in the fourth quarter, and you must be both physically and mentally ready.

2. If you miss a kick, the sooner you forget it the better.

3. Practice your steps on the sideline, using the line drill if possible.

4. Keep in touch with the game. Be ready.

5. Before you're called into the game, repeat to yourself what you must do. Be positive.

After the Game

1. Relax.

2. Jog the next day.

3. If you have game films available, analyze them and note your mistakes.

4. If you don't have access to films, keep a chart on your kicks, both good and bad. This will help you analyze bad kicks, understand what went wrong, and compensate for the error on your next kick.

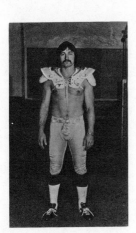

Equipment

GLOSSARY

Alignment: Positions which players line up in to begin a play.

Blitz: Play in which the defensive linebackers rush the quarterback, leaving their areas unprotected.

Cheat up: Usually occurs when an offensive player moves a bit closer to the line of scrimmage than normal in order to get a better blocking angle on the defensive man.

Closeline: A block or tackle made with the arm outstretched to simulate the effect of running into a closeline.

Coffin corner: End zone corner.

Cutback: Running situation in which the ball carrier runs in the direction called by the quarterback for a particular play, the flow of the defense cuts him off, and he has to run back against the flow to avoid being tackled.

Danger man: The first receiver who enters a linebacker's area.

Draw: Play designed to look like a pass during which the quarterback gives the ball to a running back as he drops back.

Flag: Pass route with receiver ending up heading for the flag at the corner of the field.

Flow: The direction of the play.

Gaming situation: Occurs when the defense is fairly certain of which play the offense will call, and set up to stop it.

Key: Some indication on the part of the offense that will tip off their play, or the move a particular player is going to make.

Mad dog passer: Describes the quarterback who sets up but gets pressured before he can pass. The quarterback then runs wherever he can find an opening, picking up whatever blockers he can.

Monster man: Independent defensive back on the strong side of the field.

Near back: Running back in the backfield (not slot or wing) closest to the defensive player in question.

Noseman: The defensive man who plays nose-to-nose with the offensive center.

Off side man: Player on the side of the field away from the play.

Off side play: Play to the other side of the field to the player in question.

Plug: Occurs when a lineman or middle linebacker uses his body to plug a hole and force the play elsewhere through the line.

Power sweep: Running play around the end of the line and led by both guards and a running back as blockers.

Pulling guard: The offensive guard who, on a particular play, does not block the man over him but pulls out of his position to run in front of the ballcarrier in order to block.

Red call: Call made by the quarterback after the snap when he decides to run instead of passing as intended, or by a defensive back after an interception when he needs blocking.

Release out: The movement of either the offensive or defensive linemen out of their stance.

Quick screen: Same as screen, only somewhat quicker than normal and usually to a wide receiver.

Screen: Offensive technique used with a dropback pass. The offense allows penetration, then sets up their offense behind the penetration. The quarterback passes short over the heads of the defense.

Stunting: The stunt is a defensive manoeuvre in which tackles or ends rush hard to penetrate the offensive backfield.

Trap: Blocking situation in which the off side lineman pulls behind his line and blocks a defender from the side.

Wrap-up: Tackling technique used when a defensive man uses his arms to tie a man up from behind and drive him down.

Date Due			
APR 21			